Practical and profound, *Take Good Care* is for every adult who admits intimacy into their lives. Stories that meld with Cynthia Orange's wise and insightful narrative show how it feels to be a caregiver—in all of its varied forms, with all of its rewards and challenges. This book differs from others on the subject in scope and depth, as it connects self with community and encompasses the importance of self-care, service, and nurturing compassionate children. Ultimately this book is about how to have more joy in our lives as we practice healthy caregiving.

> —**Patrick Dougherty,** licensed psychologist and author of
> *A Whole-Hearted Embrace: Finding Love at the Center of It All*

To those engaged in the challenging journey of caregiving, I recommend this outstanding book without reservation. *Take Good Care* is abundant in wisdom, practical tools, helpful stories, and—most important—the insightful compassion that every caregiver deserves and benefits from—step after step, decision upon decision.

> —**Reverend Dr. Gretchen Thompson,** hospice chaplain and
> author of *God Knows Caregiving Can Pull You Apart:*
> *12 Ways to Keep It All Together*

A deep and important look at the art of caregiving, *Take Good Care* moves us from care*taking* to care*giving* and shows us how to embrace our capacity to connect with others. Cynthia Orange's circle of care strategy is a brilliant application of Susan Silk's "Ring Theory" that we as caregivers can employ when what is meant to be a loving act overwhelms us. An essential resource for those in the outer circles as well.

> —**Harry Haroutunian, MD,** former physician director, Betty Ford
> Center, and author of *Not As Prescribed* and *Being Sober*

TAKE GOOD CARE

Finding Your Joy in
Compassionate Caregiving

CYNTHIA ORANGE

With a foreword by Susan Allen Toth, author of
No Saints around Here: A Caregiver's Days

Hazelden
Publishing

Hazelden Publishing
Center City, Minnesota 55012
hazelden.org/bookstore

ISBN: 978-1-61649-673-9

Library of Congress Cataloging-in-Publication Data is on file with the Library of
Congress.

Editor's note
Some names, details, and circumstances have been changed to protect the privacy
of those mentioned in this publication.

This publication is not intended as a substitute for the advice of health care
professionals.

Readers should be aware that websites listed in this work may have changed or
disappeared between when this work was written and when it is read.

Alcoholics Anonymous and AA are registered trademarks of Alcoholics Anonymous World Services, Inc.

21 20 19 18 17   1 2 3 4 5 6

Cover design: Terri Kinne
Interior design and typesetting: Percolator Graphic Design
Developmental editor: Sid Farrar

Author's Note

The stories excerpted throughout this book are based on actual experiences, relayed to me through interviews and conversations or in response to questionnaires distributed to caregivers and care recipients and professionals who provide counseling or other help to individuals and families dealing with caregiving issues. (These questionnaires can be found in appendix A and appendix B of this book.)

Unless otherwise noted, these stories are presented anonymously or the names have been changed to protect the privacy of the people involved. In some cases, some details have been changed or the stories are presented as composites to ensure anonymity.

Dedication

For my sister Dianne—with love, and in memory of Lee. Thank you for trusting me to share your caregiving journey.

For my grandsons, Oskar and Quin—the kindest children I know. I love being your Meema.

For my daughter, Jessica, and son-in-law, Jeff—who continue to bring such joy, wisdom, humor, and love to my life and to our family.

And for Michael, my husband and best friend—I treasure our yesterdays, embrace our todays, and welcome all our tomorrows. I love you

Contents

Foreword: Opening the Door

When I hear the word *caregiving,* I think of a particular room. It held a stark metal hospital bed, a ceiling-to-floor grabbing device, a bulky recliner borrowed from hospice, a wheelchair, a card table with two chairs, a commode bravely padded in bright blue, a desk devoured by a TV set, and an ugly CD player.

For almost two years, my much-loved husband, James, felled by Parkinson's with eventual dementia, was mostly confined to this room. Although I was very fortunate to have help, I spent lots of time there too. Even now, years after his death, I can feel James's tight grip on my arm and count his few lurching steps from the bed to the recliner, from the recliner to the wheelchair, from the little table to the shower. Once designed as a spacious bedroom for my teenage daughter, the room soon came to seem small. Suffocatingly small.

In *Take Good Care: Finding Your Joy in Compassionate Caregiving,* Cynthia Orange opened up that room. She took me up the stairs and out my front door into a larger space, a caregiving community that eventually links into an even larger world. This is a world in which anyone with a sense of connection to others is a potential giver of care. Although she pays attention to those whom we ordinarily think of as caregivers—a daughter looking after her aging father, a husband tending to the needs of a dying wife, parents trying to aid a child struggling with mental illness—she expands that definition. At some point in life, she reminds us, everyone needs help.

For Cynthia, caregiving takes many forms. A caregiver might be someone who mows a lawn for a sick friend or a willing volunteer who joins a circle of care (the author usefully graphs this concept using concentric circles moving from the primary caregivers out to people playing less vital roles). In her challenging last chapter, "Raising Compassionate Children and Paying It Forward," she lists specific ways parents can teach compassionate caregiving to their children. In fact, her whole book is a multipurpose teaching tool.

As she explains, "I also believe in my heart of hearts that care*giving* is an art—an important skill that can be learned, practiced, refined, valued, and shared."

Note those italics: care*giving*, not care*taking*. In her first chapter, "A Closer Look at Care*taking*," she lucidly describes the difference and warns readers how to avoid losing themselves when they (perhaps mistakenly) think they are helping. In chapter 3, "Balance and Boundaries," she continues this exploration. I can't imagine anyone not smiling wryly in recognition at some of her examples of how essential—and difficult—it can be to set boundaries. I love this one: "Does someone frequently keep you on the phone for over an hour even though you've said 'I have to get going' or 'I've only got a minute' at the beginning of the conversation?" After I read this, I wondered if I might learn to say, "I'm sorry, but I have an incoming message from Cynthia Orange, and she needs me to hang up."

What keep such chapters from sounding preachy are the author's frequent reassurances that she does not always successfully follow her own advice. As someone who takes much too seriously random pop-up tests with questions like "Are You a Worrier?," "Do You Have Insomnia?," or "Why Do You Hold Grudges?," I was apt at first to finish the caregiving checklists or questionnaires in this book by thinking, "Oh. That's me." But then I would read: "If you're like me, you discover that these are not 'either/or' behaviors," or "Whether I think or say them, I find that words like *always* or *never* or *if only* or all the variations of *should*, like *must* or *ought* or *supposed to*, are clues that I'm on my way to forming an unreasonable expectation." Whew.

This is not a book to make anyone feel guilty. Cynthia encourages us: "There are as many different kinds of caregiving as there are caregivers, so the lens through which you read these pages is yours alone."

A very effective lens in *Take Good Care* turns its focus on stories. Cynthia has gathered many vivid, sometimes wrenching, often consoling anecdotes and personal histories.

Their range is amazing. Demonstrating how anyone may be hit by what the author calls "Lightning Strikes," one woman and her husband were happily kayaking and camping when the husband became ill. They headed to shore. Within days, he was diagnosed with advanced pancreatic cancer. His wife: "I can't believe how fast life can change. It seems like I was kayaking and laughing with him one moment, and planning his memorial service the next." In this clear-eyed chapter, Cynthia offers what preparation is possible for such emergencies. For instance, she gives thorough instructions about assembling an In Case of Emergency (ICE) card, with all relevant information that can save both a caregiver and a care receiver valuable time. I immediately reviewed my own ICE card, which I carry in my billfold, to see if it was up to date. (I needed to make a few additions.)

In a chapter devoted to brain disorders, including dementia in its different forms, caregivers share compelling stories about their coping strategies. Some are as simple as using Post-it Notes or creating unique picture albums. Others involve the trickiness of understanding or negotiating their own limits. One caregiver painfully learns: "For the sake of my sanity and our relationship, I need to limit my visits to two a week unless there's an emergency." For me, the most poignant story is a daughter's report from her mother's descent into Alzheimer's: "So much joy in simple things. I also found a blanket with a picture of two beautiful little children with wings. When I brought it to her, she grabbed it and said, 'Come to Grandma,' as though they were real children. She loved that blanket, and it covered her legs in the casket when she died."

This book is a wise, wide-ranging compendium of such anecdotes, stories, suggestions, questionnaires, and graphic aids—but it is much more than that. Cynthia invites her readers to join in a universal vision of caring for others, with all the unexpected and even unwanted variables caregiving includes.

Take Good Care affirms that we are all part of the fallible and mortal human family. We need to know how to give care, for ourselves as well as others, and how to receive it. It assures us that we are not alone. So for any new caregiver who feels psychologically or physically trapped in a small room, this book is here to help lead you out.

Susan Allen Toth
Author of *No Saints around Here: A Caregiver's Days*

Prologue

When a little girl began playing the first notes of her piece at our grandsons' last Christmas piano recital, I whispered excitedly to Michael, "It's 'Suzy Snowflake'—my ballet song!" Though it had been over five decades, the memory was clear, and I could still hear the words of the song in my head. I was ten, the age of our twin grandsons, and my friend Linda and I were performing the dance for our fourth-grade talent show.

I was excited but confident as the record started, and Rosemary Clooney sang the opening lines as we stepped onto the auditorium stage, looking adorable, I'm sure, in our white tutus. "Here comes Suzy Snowflake, dressed in a snow-white gown." Our entrance went well, but then disaster struck. When I extended my hands overhead and bent down over my pointed toe, ready for the "Tap, tap, tappin' at your windowpane" move, I happened to look up to see Linda doing some sort of a pirouette. Although I knew our dance number perfectly, instead of carrying on as we had been taught, I tuned into Linda's wrong move and, in a futile attempt to fix things, tried to follow her spin and the mishmash ballet that followed it. I was worried about her—about both of us—looking stupid, and I didn't want her to get angry or not like me if I didn't pretend she was right. Then, of course, even though I knew better, I began to doubt myself and my abilities. As I recall, my career as a ballerina was short-lived, and I gave up on dance altogether after that experience.

In the retelling of this story to my husband, I had one of those aha moments. By the ripe age of ten, my life as a codependent care-*taker* had already begun.

Introduction

Caregiving often calls us to lean into love we didn't know possible.
—TIA WALKER, *THE INSPIRED CAREGIVER*[1]

According to the 2015 report *Caregiving in the U.S.* by the National Alliance for Caregiving and the AARP Public Policy Institute,[2] nearly 44 million adults in this country provide personal assistance for family members with disabilities or other care needs. As this report states, and as you'll discover from the variety of voices in this book, "Caregivers are as diverse as the United States as a whole: they come from every age, gender, socioeconomic, and racial/ethnic group."

Although they are not included in the above statistic, I'm guessing that the numbers are also great for the individuals or teams of family members, friends, and coworkers who provide necessary shorter-term care for an acquaintance, friend, or loved one in need, as well as members of civic, Twelve Step, religious, or other organizations providing mutual support to their peers. This person in need could be someone who requires extra care and support because of things like the physical and mental effects of aging, depression, surgery, an accident, a serious illness, a trauma of some sort, a deep loss, recovery from alcohol or other drug addiction, or other significant life event. And the circle of care expands even further when we consider all the professionals who care for us on a daily basis.

There are also those countless everyday times when we give "spontaneous" care or support to someone who has an emotional problem, who is facing an upsetting work or family issue, or who may feel overwhelmed, sad, scared, or lonely. How we respond to those in need can leave us with a feeling of either joy and fulfillment or emptiness and resentment.

When it comes to our spouses or partners, our children, or our parents, we may feel that caregiving "chooses" us. In other situations, we may choose caregiving. Healthy caregiving is the balanced act of reaching out to others with an open heart and helping hand that connects us to the better parts of ourselves as we connect to those in need and to the community that surrounds them. Approached realistically—with intention, support, and a good mixture of patience, humor, and flexibility—it can be a time of joy and discovery and a chance to practice important life skills that prove valuable in a variety of situations. Compassionate caregiving is also an opportunity to engage in service work as we make or deepen more honest, open, and balanced relationships.

In contrast to healthy care*giving*, care*taking* (which is explained in more detail on the next page and throughout this book) can result in an uneven "one up/one down" relationship that risks leaving both people feeling depleted, unhappy, and resentful. While not dismissing the many and oft-discussed difficulties, challenges, and burdens of caregiving, this book will help readers focus on the often-hidden gifts that caregivers receive when they reach out to others in a loving and mutually beneficial way that can leave both people feeling nourished and respected.

In addition, this book offers support, encouragement, and self-care suggestions for all caregivers—those who face the ongoing challenges of caring for a loved one, patient, or client on a day-to-day basis, as well as those who lend an occasional hand to give care to someone in need. It includes up-to-date research and resources, as well as real-life stories from both caregivers and care receivers who offer practical tips and guidance on what has worked for them and what hasn't worked as well. I believe we learn best through stories, and I am forever grateful for the wise and courageous voices heard in this book. It was often difficult for these men and women to share their experiences, but they did so in order to help others. Their words are insightful, sometimes painful, sometimes funny, but always honest.

As many of you may have already discovered, caregiving isn't something that happens just one time or with just one person. We have the opportunity to give and receive care throughout our entire lives, so I'm hoping the information in this book will benefit experienced caregivers as well as readers who may be new to caregiving. But before we delve more deeply into the difficulties, benefits, and emotional ups and downs that come with giving care, I want to talk a bit about terminology.

As a writer, I know how easy it is to get hung up on words, labels, and definitions—especially when it comes to sometimes loaded or complex terms like *codependent* or *caretaker* (as opposed to *caregiver*). Even words like *love* can get overused and stretched until they become a little hollow, as in "*love* ya, babe," yet we aren't about to abandon such an important expression of endearment. Besides, we each know what we mean and what we want to convey when we use it.

This is why I like the Zen saying "Words are like fingers pointing at the moon." While we can't learn anything about the moon by focusing on the finger, words do come in handy when we're trying to describe the beauty of a full moon rising over a serene landscape. Then it's up to each of us to paint our own mental picture of the scene. In the same way, words can direct us to important concepts or in the case of this book, *behaviors*—and carve the way to new ideas, deeper understandings, and individual truths.

To get the most out of this book, I think it's important to make sure we're speaking the same language, so I want to explain how the words *codependency* and *caretaker* (as contrasted with *caregiver*) will be used in these pages.

What Is Codependency and What Does It Have to Do with Caring for Someone?

If you have difficulty with the term *codependency*, know that you are not alone. I've always had trouble with it too. As a close friend asked me the other day, "Aren't we all dependent on each other to some degree? Isn't that an important part of being in relationships? Isn't being able to depend on a trusted friend a *good* thing?"

She's right, of course. If you look up the prefix *co-* in the dictionary, you find it means things like "mutual" or "joint," so if we take the word literally, it sounds like just what she's describing. But, like many words, *codependency* is not usually used in the literal sense. And often, this behavior is more a solo than a joint venture.

To put it simply, I would describe *codependency* as the word is commonly used today as the *out-of-balance behavior of someone who is overinvolved* in another person's life. Melody Beattie is credited for popularizing the term in her 1986 best-selling book *Codependent No More,* in which she describes codependents as people who become so obsessed with other people's feelings and behaviors that they—in an effort to control or fix them—lose sight of their own feelings and actions.

My ten-year-old grandson gave me a new perspective on the issue of control when he came down with a flu bug last Thanksgiving. He had so looked forward to the school holiday and a long weekend to be with family and play with his twin brother and their friends. "I don't *want* to be sick, Meema," he told me sadly when I went to check on him. In an effort to console him, I said, "But just think, honey. If you're still sick tomorrow, we can give you all the attention. You can be the boss of all of us!" His response was quick and firm. "That doesn't sound like fun at all, Meema. Being everybody's boss sounds like *way* too much responsibility." My grandson is right. While the fantasy of being the "boss" might at first seem appealing, taking complete control wouldn't be that much fun in the long run. And it isn't very realistic.

As you'll learn in future chapters, giving up the illusion of control is an integral step in achieving a healthy balance in relationships. While it is true that being loving, giving, and nurturing are admirable qualities, it's important to balance that reality with taking time to love and nurture ourselves too—especially in the types of caregiving relationships that will be discussed in these pages. Often that means letting go of the idea that we have the power to change anyone.

You may have heard the old saying "You can lead a horse to water, but you can't make it drink." In other words, we can guide and even nag others, but—as much as we might try and as good as we think we might be at it—we can't script their lives or control how they will act or react. We can plot and plan, yet the unexpected still happens. We can buckle our own and our children's and grandchildren's seat belts and drive as carefully as possible, but we have no control over the careless driver who veers into our lane and smashes into our car. Just as we have no control over diseases like cancer, diabetes, Parkinson's disease, Alzheimer's disease, or addiction that may strike someone we care about deeply.

I italicized the word *overinvolved* in my definition of codependency for a reason. If we are the primary caregiver for someone who has a serious illness or injury or physical or mental condition that requires significant—maybe even full-time—attention for whatever length of time, of course we need to be greatly involved in his or her life and care, often to the point of exhaustion. Some of us reach that point sooner than others; others may never reach it. Even though the caregiving needs may be similar, we are all different, with different limitations, support systems, and resources, and this book takes that into account.

But I think we know when something feels *out of balance*, which is why I included that element in my description. There's a joke in Twelve Step circles about how you know you're a codependent when you have a near-death experience and someone else's life flashes before your eyes. It is often easier, and I would argue sometimes necessary, to put another's needs ahead of our own, but if we do that day after day, hour after hour without also taking care of ourselves, we risk losing sight of who we are and what *our* needs are independent from our loved ones. That is why this book will, among other things, stress the need for healthy balance and boundaries and the importance of good self-care.

What Is the Difference between
Caretaking and Caregiving?

I think of caretaking as codependency's close cousin. However, while there has been a trend to think of codependency as a pathological disease that requires treatment, I don't view caretaking through that same lens in this book. While many caretaking behaviors may be similar to codependent behaviors, my aim is to normalize them somewhat because I believe we all have a tendency to caretake from time to time. As readers will discover, it is when these tendencies become extreme or automatic that we find ourselves giving so much to so many so often that we risk losing sight of ourselves in the process.

Although the words caretaking and caregiving are often used interchangeably, I think it is useful to make a distinction and important to define what I mean by these terms at the outset since we will be exploring the many aspects of these behaviors throughout this book.

To understand the difference between caretaking and caregiving, focus for a minute on the words take and give. Caretakers often have a tendency to swoop in to take charge, take over, or take control of a situation or person in an effort to fix a situation or even a person— often without being asked or without even realizing they're doing it. When we jump in to rescue someone who doesn't need or want to be rescued, we run the risk of capsizing the whole "relationship boat," possibly straining a relationship or even sinking a friendship.

Of course, there are times of crisis when "swooping in" is just what may be necessary. When someone close to us experiences a health emergency, an accident, a fire or natural disaster, a sudden death in the family, or some other sudden and unexpected catastrophe, the person or persons most affected may be temporarily numb—paralyzed by grief or uncertainty as to where to turn or what to do. But, here again, it comes back to balance and boundaries. Most of us know in our hearts if we are the appropriate ones to rush to the aid of a friend or family member in critical need of help.

For example, my mom died suddenly, only three days after she was diagnosed with stage IV lung cancer. She was a nonsmoker who, at eighty-three, bowled on two leagues and exercised at least three times a week—so you can imagine how shocked we were by her unexpected death. My siblings lived elsewhere, so I was the in-town primary caregiver. Knowing this, and knowing that relatives would be staying with us, a dear friend arrived at our doorstep, cleaning supplies in hand, to prepare our house for guests. She instinctively realized what I needed before I did. This was a considerate gesture of compassion that I shall long remember. This was *caregiving* in action where a trusted friend *gave* from the deep well of love she had for me and my family, knowing I would have done the same for her. However, had this been someone I wasn't that close to, I would have felt awkward or "invaded" at such a time of deep and private emotion.

There's no denying that caring for others can make us feel good about ourselves. That's only natural. As I said before, reaching out to others with an open heart and helping hand can bring out the best in us. But things get a little murky when the act of giving care is so ego driven that we don't feel good about ourselves *unless* we're doing something for someone else. Speaking from my own experience, care*takers* need to be needed; they need to be liked. When I'm in care*taker* mode, I've caught myself going out of my way to do something I don't want to do for someone I don't even like because I want them to think highly of me. In such instances, caring for others becomes more about me than them. Of course, now that I'm a grown-up, I am able to put my feelings and needs aside and help everyone—friend and foe alike—in a pure spirit of love and generosity. And if you believe that . . .

A psychologist friend of mine—one of the wisest women I know—talks about the seductiveness of wanting to be the "special one." Here's how she put it:

It's a struggle not to define our worth by how much others need us. It's everywhere in our culture—in medicine, in politics, in teaching, everywhere—especially when others feed that tendency and project that image by telling us how wonderful and extraordinary we are. Hopefully, when we come to recognize that what people think—both negatively and positively—is not necessarily the way things really are, we let go of the fierce need to be the special one.

To sum up this discussion of how the terms care*taking* and care*giving* are used in this book, I think it helps to think of care*taking* as the out-of-balance and "self-centered" behaviors that reflect a person's deep need to be in control and accepted. On the other hand, care*giving* consists of more balanced behaviors that reflect compassion and concern for others. You might say that care*taking* is more about getting love, while care*giving* is more about giving it.

If you're like me, you discover that these are not "either/or" behaviors. I find that I can be the poster girl for healthy and compassionate caregiving one day and an example of an unhealthy, controlling, and out-of-balance caretaker on another day, depending on the circumstance or the person. I confess that my caretaker within most often emerges when caring for a close friend or family member. But I'm getting better at recognizing those caretaking and controlling tendencies when they occur. Then I dust myself off, make amends, and remind myself of what I've learned and share in this book about the importance of healthy boundaries and mutual respect, maintaining balance, letting go of the need to control, and the need to practice good self-care.

The Goals of This Book

One of the ongoing joys of my life is co-facilitating a caregivers' group. Several of the members care for aging parents with Alzheimer's or other health challenges; others care for seriously ill family members or friends. Some members have been with the group since it began over five years ago. Some leave when their loved one dies;

some when their loved one recovers. Some rejoin when a cancer or condition recurs or worsens. And the door is always open to welcome new members who enter with new stories and caregiving concerns.

I love and gain so much from this community of brave souls who gather once a month for mutual support. The only rule is "What's said in the room stays in the room." It's a place where caregivers can share their feelings and fears without having to worry about being judged or advised or told what to do or not do, what to feel or not feel. They can be angry. They can be tired. They can swear if they need to and cry if they want to. And so often we find ourselves erupting into unexpected laughter. As one member described it:

> The group really helps because it gives me permission and freedom to say whatever I need to say. There is sanctuary and safety in the group. We celebrate together. Cry together. Everyone's situation is unique, yet the same in many ways. There is strength in the common struggle.

While the overall goal of this book is to help readers become more intentional and self-aware when they give care to others, another important goal is to provide "strength in the common struggle"—to welcome you into a community where you can find information, guidance, comfort, and support from those who "have been there and done that." Your caregiving experience is unique to you, so some suggestions or tips might appeal to you more than others. As they say in Twelve Step groups, "Take what you need and leave the rest," although I would add, "or share the rest if you want to."

I don't pretend to have all the answers, but I hope that by sharing the information, resources, and stories I've gathered for this book, I've helped you in your own quest to find ways to take better care of yourself as you take tender care of someone else. In addition to helping you sort out the differences between codependent caretak-ing and compassionate caregiving, between self-care and "other care," I hope this book will also be a prevention tool.

Caregivers, like anyone else who juggles the often-overwhelming responsibilities and challenges of life, are vulnerable to stress-related illnesses, to depression, and to addiction or other unhealthy behaviors. If readers use a suggestion contained in this book at a time of stress or confusion instead of pouring a drink, popping a pill, or engaging in some other potentially harmful behavior, it will have done its job.

While many studies address the physical and psychological toll that caregiving can take, others, like the five-year study by researchers at three universities conducted by psychology professor Michael Poulin, show how helping others can actually protect our health by lessening the negative effects of stress and lengthening our lives.[3] It is my hope that readers will experience these same benefits as they learn to distinguish stress-laden care*taking* from healthy care*giving* so they can achieve more balance in their lives as busy care*givers*. That's why much of this book is about how to nurture and nourish yourself, how to breathe deeply, slow down, and explore ways to carve out more time for yourself and the activities that so often get overlooked when caring for others. When we take good care of ourselves, we can create a reservoir of energy, patience, and love that will be there when we need it.

As cliché as the African saying has become, it really does "take a village" when we're trying to do everything we need to get done in a day plus make time for helping others. It was an important step in the right direction when support groups started calling what happened at their meetings "mutual help" instead of "self-help." If there is one thing the many millions of people who belong to these groups all over the world have learned, it is the importance of asking for and giving help when it is needed. One of the goals of this book is to help you expand the circles of support you have in place and to guide you in creating support systems and networks if none currently exist. I have included a list of helpful organizations, books, and websites at the end of the book.

There are as many different kinds of caring relationships as there are caregivers, so the lens through which you read these pages is yours alone. Whether you give care to one person who is seriously ill or incapacitated or to several people on a more casual helping basis, I think you can benefit from the information contained in this book and from learning what others have so generously shared. As you ponder the contents, I urge you to consider what adjustments you might make and what elements of self-care you might incorporate in order to achieve a saner and healthier balance. After all, isn't that what we all want?

Knowledge is an important step in any journey, and it is a step *forward*. It is my wish that you will find hope and comfort in these pages as well as helpful information you can put to good use. I hope you will emerge convinced that you do not travel alone.

What's Ahead

As you digest the information in these pages and read the honest, poignant, sometimes-funny stories told by real caregivers, try to think of breathing in, then breathing out. In a way, that's what this book does as it moves from internal self-reflection to an external "self to community" connection.

We begin by looking within as we learn more about the differences between care*taking* and care*giving* and take an honest look on which side of the balance sheet our caring behaviors most often fall. I say "most often," because as I stress throughout the book, caregiving is a fluid process, and it's common to slide back and forth on the caring continuum.

As we move along that continuum, we learn the importance of embracing imperfection. We examine the mixed messages we may have received about caring for others and talk about curbing our expectations and defusing resentments. Then we discuss the different types of boundaries and the critical need for healthy balance and boundaries as we learn how to set and maintain reasonable limits in our lives. Next we move toward others, as we discover how to create "circles of care" and locate our place in such circles.

Compassion is at the heart of healthy caregiving, which is why we dig into the subject by taking a look at the difference between sympathy, empathy, compassion, and what I call "boundaried" empathy and "empathetic" compassion. As you'll see, when I talk about compassion, I don't just mean compassion for others—I mean compassion for self as well. Such tenderness toward self requires diligent self-care practices.

Practicing good self-care as described in these pages opens the door to the joys that healthy caregiving can bring and prepares us for the many caring challenges that may come our way—challenges that are discussed in the latter part of the book.

The book concludes by "breathing out," moving from self to other to community as we look at the ways we might foster compassion in children and think about things we can do to "pay it forward" as we reach out to help those beyond our immediate circle of care.

Throughout the book, you'll also find practical tools and guides, many of which are included in the appendixes for your use and duplication. There are evocative questions to help you assess and think about your own caregiving practices. Along with the numerous stories and tips from other caregivers, you'll find advice from experts as well as my own suggestions and examples for ways that might make your own caregiving experiences less stressful and more joyful.

So let the journey begin.

CHAPTER 1

A Closer Look at Caretaking

Giving myself away and being stingy are not my only options. I can share myself. Yet to share myself, I have to have a self to share.
—ANNE WILSON SCHAEF, *MEDITATIONS FOR WOMEN WHO DO TOO MUCH*[1]

I have this friend who is the biggest-hearted person I know. Alex is always at the ready to help a friend or even a casual acquaintance when he thinks help is needed. He'll clear trails for hiking or cross-country skiing; chop and stack wood at someone's cabin so they'll have it when the weather turns; help a friend move across town or across the country; paint walls; clip articles and send them to me when he knows I'm working on a project; call to check in when someone in our family is sick or troubled. And he does these deeds with patience and good humor.

If you had the energy to follow Alex around for a day or two, it might be easy to conclude that all that *giving* seems out of balance—more like the care*taking* described in the introduction. But he still finds lots of time for his wife and kids and grandkids. He meditates and exercises and goes to his Twelve Step meetings faithfully. Being of service is an important part of his recovery, so what might feel like care*taking* to others no doubt feels like care*giving* to him.

The point of this story—and this chapter—is that it is up to each of us to figure out for ourselves if or when caring for others is consuming us or feeding us. I think it helps to picture a continuum of care, with "care-aholics" at one extreme and saints at the other. Most of us operate somewhere in the murky middle ground, depending on the person we're caring for, the situation, the day, or the mood (theirs and ours). We're all human beings united in our imperfection, and even the most compassionate of caregivers can stumble, doing or saying something awkward or reacting with impatience or anger—especially when we're overwhelmed or exhausted.

Whether doing a simple favor for a stranger or providing long-term care for a loved one, we've all more than likely exhibited some care*taking* behaviors at one time or another. This chapter is about identifying those behaviors when they arise. (We'll work on dealing with them in future chapters.)

This process of identification is an exercise in self-awareness. When I did an Internet search for *self-awareness* just now, it took only seconds for Google to tell me it was a noun that means "conscious knowledge of one's own character, feelings, motives, and desires." While understanding what makes us tick and why we do what we do is no guarantee that we'll alter our behavior, it is an important step in accepting responsibility for our actions. Owning our actions and reactions helps us decide which ones warrant attention—which ones we may want to try to change, curb, limit, or forgive.

Acknowledging the Care*taker* Within

Have you ever caught yourself doing something for a child (or an adult, for that matter) that they were perfectly capable of doing themselves? Have you found yourself blurting out a favor—perhaps an over-the-top offer of help, money, lodging, or transportation—because you assumed someone needed such assistance? Have you ever said yes to an invitation or request and regretted it even before the word was out of your mouth because you felt obligated, guilt-tripped, or pressured? I sure have.

If you look at the chart of caring behaviors on pages 16–18, you'll see that the actions I just described would lean more toward care*taking* than care*giving.* I didn't have to work too hard to compile this list. I just had to objectively reflect on my own behaviors and relationships and record how I've acted and reacted toward others when my life has seemed in balance and when it's seemed out of whack. As Susan has learned, this process of honest self-reflection can help us more easily see the red flags when they begin to rise.

SUSAN'S STORY

I would define myself as a codependent caretaker. Although I attend regular Al-Anon meetings, I still find myself attempting to give help when it has not been requested. For example, when my granddaughter and her partner were purchasing a home, they talked about carpeting a couple of areas over the existing wood floors. I found myself printing articles about dust mites in carpet and how much healthier wood floors are. Thanks to Al-Anon, I never gave them copies of any of the articles—yet my self-absorption with other people's problems and circumstances continue to be a challenge for me.

When I'm feeling vulnerable or obsessing about an uncomfortable interaction, it helps me to revisit this list to see if some of my emotions have something to do with giving or receiving care. I might have been at my care*giver* best at the same time a friend is in care*taker* mode. Or vice versa—I might feel some pushback from someone because I'm giving unsolicited advice or being a tad judgmental about something they've said or done.

I urge you to take some time to look over the following chart and honestly think about your own tendencies when it comes to giving care. As I've stressed, since our experiences and situations differ, our reactions to this exercise will also differ. Like me, you may also find you can dance from one side of the chart to the other. And while the descriptions of "often," "frequently," or "usually" may not apply, some behaviors may be familiar to you.

As I've said, it is often necessary for those who care for someone who is seriously ill or disabled to become more care*taker* than care*giver,* and we'll talk more about those particular situations in later chapters. But I think anyone who lends a helping hand can benefit from gaining a better understanding of their own motives, actions, and reactions when it comes to giving care. More important, I think it is extremely helpful for all of us to know our individual limitations—when caring for someone is swallowing us up to the point where we are risking our own health and well-being.

But for now, just think about how you generally operate when you perform an act of caring, no matter how small the kindness or how big the sacrifice. Which of the following characteristics most closely reflects your own caring behaviors?

Some Common Characteristics of Caretakers and Caregivers

Caretakers	Caregivers
Often need to be needed	Want to be of help
Have a need or desire to fix	Support others in problem solving
Like to be the "special one"	Are usually good team players
Often try to control a person or situation	Are content to be helpers
Often try to manipulate	Try to cooperate
Often struggle with low self-esteem	Usually have a healthy sense of self
Often overstep or disregard boundaries	Respect boundaries (their own and others')
Have difficulty saying no	Can gracefully decline an invitation or request when it is necessary to do so

Caretakers	Caregivers
Tend to put others' needs above their own	Practice good self-care
Are often judgmental and critical	Are usually accepting and nonjudgmental
Often feel responsible for others' needs and feelings	Understand that they are only responsible for their *own* actions and feelings
Often "give to get"—i.e., help others out of a need to be thanked, liked, accepted, etc.	Act out of compassion and concern for others with no "strings attached"
Often have difficulty making decisions	Are not usually second-guessers
Frequently have lives out of balance	Try to live a balanced life
Are often "people pleasers"	Have a healthy respect for self *and* others
Are often poor listeners	Are usually attentive and "active" listeners
Have trouble setting and honoring priorities	Try to set and maintain priorities
Are often resentful	Are usually grateful
Often adopt an attitude of self-sacrifice	Try to maintain a spirit of generosity
Frequently lavish praise on others	Are genuine in their admiration and praise

Caretakers	Caregivers
Have a tendency to get overly involved in another person's life or problems	Maintain appropriate boundaries
Often offer advice or help without being asked	Maintain appropriate boundaries
Often have "uneven," one-up/ one-down relationships	Thrive on healthy relationships that have a good balance of "give and take"
Often assume they know what's best; are invested in being right regarding someone's care choices and may argue their point of view (even when they weren't asked for their opinion)	Respect another's opinions and choices and accept that person's decisions about their own care (even though they may disagree with them)

I suggest you make a copy of this chart so you can keep it handy and refer to it frequently as you read this book. It is in appendix C to make it easier for you to reproduce. Go ahead and mark it up, checking off the behaviors that ring true. Revisit it when a caregiving opportunity arises and see if anything has shifted. If possible, use it as a way to check in with yourself and your feelings before acting or reacting.

I heard once that self-awareness is the first step toward change. When we realize and admit that our lives are out of balance, we can begin to look beyond ourselves to get the help *we* need. As you'll learn in future pages, an important piece of care*giving* is learning how and when to ask for and accept care ourselves so we can more effectively care for others.

Here's what Rita discovered when she took an honest look at her care*taker* tendencies.

RITA'S STORY

When my kids were little (and, if I am truly honest, all the while they lived at home), I now know that I was more codependent caretaker than caregiver. I think they would be the first to say I often "hovered" more than mothered, wanting to monitor or control their actions and activities, their choice of friends, the subjects they chose to take in high school . . . I was able to detach more when they left for college, but even now I still find myself calling too often to check in (or on?). I'm working hard at not being so intrusive and worked up the courage to ask them what feels like a comfortable middle ground of connection to them. "Short texts are great, Mom. And let us call you once in a while so it feels more even and less obligatory." So I'm doing better at letting go   not obsessing about them every minute of the day and "letting them" do things for me. Amazing how much time that frees up!

However, the other day I caught myself caretaking my husband when I said, "You haven't seen Allen for a long time. Why don't you call and see if he wants to go out for lunch with you?" Right after I suggested this, I blurted out, "Oh my god—the kids are grown up and on their own, and now I'm making play dates for YOU!" We both had a good laugh and were able to see my moment of clarity as evidence that I'm making some progress in my journey of self-awareness. It's a matter of baby steps, right?

As Rita continues to discover, moving from care*taking* to care*giving* is, like all life journeys, a matter of progress, *not* perfection.

Embracing Imperfection

Perfectionism is a trait that often tugs at the sleeves of many codependent caretakers. It gets mixed in with our need to be needed, to be accepted, to be loved, and to be affirmed as worthy and worthwhile. Perfectionists usually operate in a world of illusion. We judge ourselves by impossible standards and berate ourselves when we fail to meet our unreachable goals. We drive ourselves crazy rushing about trying to be the perfect partner, parent, employee, daughter or son, friend, and, of course, the perfect caring person.

Perfectionism ultimately leads to disappointment because perfectionists are never satisfied. They live in an "if only," "less than," and "should be" world where success is always around the corner, always out of reach.

I never viewed myself as a perfectionist because I pictured a perfectionist as a person with an immaculate house and a sixty-hour-per-week job that they handled with ease while keeping their home and social life in perfect balance. Since it takes very little arm twisting for a friend to lure me away from housecleaning or my office, I did not fit my definition of a perfectionist. I have come to realize, however, that I *was* a perfectionist when it came to relationships. I set impossible standards for myself, for my friends, and for my little family; then I'd get distressed when all of us fell short of my lofty expectations. My pursuit of interpersonal excellence was a joyless journey, and I am much happier now that I see myself and my friends as "perfectly adequate."

Being (or trying to be) the perfect mother, friend, and relative often made me feel generous, sensitive, and caring. However, I also felt resentful and unappreciated at times and personally depleted because I rushed to care for everyone else instead of pausing to care for myself. I felt guilty if I forgot a birthday or important anniversary and disappointed when others didn't return my nurturing gestures. Thanks to a great therapist and some honest heart-to-heart talks with loved ones, I know now that my devotion often made others uncomfortable because it was so out of balance in terms of what they were willing or able to give back. I discovered, for example, that it was more important to simply be present with my friends and less important to remember that their aunt Martha twice removed was having eye surgery.

I also learned that deep friendship happens when people are willing to be mutually vulnerable with each other. My friends didn't want or expect me to be Mother Teresa. They were *perfectly* willing to accept me as *me,* in all my splendid imperfection. Being imperfect, of course, means that I can still trip up and slip back into a state of self-doubt and neediness, but at least I can recognize and own that now when it happens. I think of care*giving* as a practice like meditation and exercise. And, contrary to the old saying, practice does *not* "make perfect." I'm a lousy meditator, a well-intentioned but inconsistent exerciser, and an imperfect caregiver. But I keep working at it with the comfort of knowing that making progress is more realistic (and less stressful) than trying to attain perfection.

One of the things that helped me better understand and accept myself as a "relationship perfectionist" and care*taker* was learning how our feelings result from the distorted messages we give ourselves. This idea that our attitudes direct our feelings is at the heart of cognitive therapy. In the 1980s, I was given a book on the subject that I've mentioned in other writing I've done and that I still use today—*Feeling Good: The New Mood Therapy* by psychiatrist Dr. David Burns.[2] Evidently, others feel the same way about this book since it's sold over three million copies. Burns explains that our thoughts or perceptions (our "cognitions") often have more to do with how we feel than what is actually happening in our lives.

When I went through a particularly difficult time, I didn't realize how distorted my thinking was. *I* made sense to *me.* Instead of looking inward for the cause of my unhappiness, I convinced myself (and often others) that it was the weather or my spouse or my boss or some other external force that was the problem. After some time, I felt like a curtain had been lifted. I was both elated and terrified to realize how powerful my thoughts were, and how negative or distorted thoughts—what recovering alcoholics might call "stinking thinking"—could paralyze me.

When we slip into distorted thinking, we have a tendency to see the world as black and white. We believe things always happen *to* us; we usually see the negative in something or transform positive experiences into negative ones. Burns says that distorted thinkers are often convinced other people are looking down on them and jump to negative conclusions about what others are thinking or feeling. (If a friend doesn't call or if someone isn't paying close enough attention to us, they *must* hate us.) Distorted thinkers think at the extremes. They might magnify their faults out of proportion while they play down any strengths they have. They may also mistake their emotions for facts. It's an "I feel, therefore it is" approach to life. (If I'm angry with you, you *must* have done something contrary.) Burns says distorted thinkers also have a "shouldy" approach to life, often beating themselves up for what they think they should and shouldn't do, ultimately creating self-loathing, shame, and guilt because they feel they are constantly falling short of their expectations. When I get in this state of mind, I try to remember the slogan I heard years ago: "Don't 'should' all over yourself!"

Dr. Burns suggests that perfectionists make a list of the advantages and disadvantages of being perfectionistic. He predicts that when they see how the disadvantages (it makes me nervous; I'm afraid of making a mistake; I get self-critical; I can't relax; it makes me impatient with others; it keeps me from taking risks; it isn't any fun; it makes me inefficient; it helps me procrastinate) can outweigh any advantages (it motivates me to work harder to reach my goals), they will relax a bit and not try so desperately to be perfect.

Progress, not perfection. Progress, not perfection. Say it with feeling; capture the rhythm of the phrase. It chugs along like the little engine that could in the old children's story. (Notice it wasn't the little engine that *should*.) The goal for caretakers—the goal for everyone, for that matter—is to move forward, one day, one experience, and yes, even one mistake, at a time.

Giving to Get

If you study the common characteristics of care*takers* as set forth in the chart on pages 16–18, you'll notice that many describe or refer to personal *need*. Caretakers often *need* to be needed, to be accepted, to be affirmed as being okay. They want to be noticed and liked, so they often struggle to gain control and visibility. Instead of looking within for fulfillment, they often look to others to fill voids in their own lives. As mentioned, while helping others certainly can feed us, giving care and doing favors with the expectation that our doing so will gain us love and friends and self-esteem can be a recipe for disappointment.

I blame the idea of giving to get on Santa Claus. Most of us were probably told as children, "Be nice and Santa will bring you presents." We learn very early on that our actions will be rewarded *if* we behave properly. From a child's perspective, this can translate into "The nicer I am, the more I'll get."

As I've discovered myself, and as others have described to me, trying to "buy" love and attention through caretaking when we're feeling lonely and invisible usually backfires. Ned, the husband of a woman who struggles with an anxiety disorder, describes how he discovered his own caretaker within.

NED'S STORY

Before she was diagnosed, I thought my spouse's obsessive need to fill her time with work and house projects or exercise was a way to avoid me. Neither of us realized her compulsive behavior was related to an anxiety disorder. I often complained that I became the last thing on her list of priorities—if I made the list at all. But instead of tending to my own life, I tried to control her and her schedule, and I got overinvolved in our kids' lives. I poured all my energy into the lives of my family and friends. I devoted myself to others and expected them to give me the same time and attention in return. I became the classic codependent caretaker. And I was miserable. I think I thought things would change if she saw how wonderful I was.

Caretakers often live in an "if I do or say this, then this will happen" world of expectation, which more often than not results in disappointment and even anger. As they say in Twelve Step circles, an expectation is a premeditated resentment. This is what Jasmine found when she gave a gift, thinking she would get something of equal value back.

JASMINE'S STORY

I surprised my friend for his thirtieth birthday by getting us expensive tickets to a rock concert because I knew he loved the band that was in town. Instead of reacting with the excitement I had anticipated, he said, "I wish you had checked with me first. I had plans for that night, but I'll see if I can change them." He was able to go, and we had an okay time, but I realized my evening was tainted because I was disappointed in his initial reaction. Hell, I didn't even like that band; I just wanted to please him. He didn't even offer to pay for parking. He did take me out for lunch on my thirtieth two months later, but it felt sort of imbalanced after what I had spent on him.

When we move from care*taking* to care*giving*, we throw out the "scales of justice" and accept that human interactions aren't always even-steven. We can drive ourselves crazy if we give a gift, do a favor, or extend an invitation expecting that the gift receiver will return our gesture with something of equal value. Here's how Cecile decided to deal with this issue.

CECILE'S STORY

I've been close friends with Lisa for almost fifty years. We've been through a lot together—marriages, kids, divorces, remarriages, and deaths of loved ones. I'm usually the one who calls to check in, and it used to really bother me that I was doing most of the "work" in the friendship. It was easy for me to feel resentful. Then we'd connect, and it felt like no time had passed even if we hadn't talked for a couple of months. She's always happy to hear

from me. We'll laugh and cry and chat for hours. I love her and
miss her and know she loves me and misses me and would do
anything for me. I've accepted that we're just different when it
comes to human interactions and that I have a choice. I could feel
sorry for myself and be stubborn, taking a stance of "I won't be
the first to call this time," or I can do as I choose to do—call her
when I feel the urge and celebrate the fact that this is a friendship
to cherish, even if it isn't a perfectly "balanced" one. It's worth a
little extra effort on my part.

Healthy caregiving isn't about letting go of all expectations; it's about sorting out reasonable expectations from unreasonable ones. It's reasonable to expect our loved ones and friends to listen to us attentively when we are sharing something important to us. It's unreasonable for us to expect people to be mind readers and know what we're thinking or feeling or needing if we don't express our thoughts and feelings or communicate our needs.

Unmet expectations can leave us feeling disappointed and unhappy. The very word *disappointment* makes me squirm, to say nothing of the emotion itself. It releases a chorus of critical voices inside my head—my dad, a teacher, a boss, or a friend letting me know I hadn't lived up to *their* expectations. Often the loudest voice is my own—the internal critic that judges harshly, berating me for not being better, for not saying the "right" thing, for not meeting the unreasonable expectations I often set for myself.

Here's where self-awareness comes in once again. Now when I feel disappointed in a person (or in myself), it's usually a clue that my expectations might be unrealistic and out of alignment with the present reality. It's also a clue that I may be caretaking. Then I try to stop, breathe, reflect, and let go of any unrealistic expectations I may be harboring.

Unreasonable expectations can block us from enjoying close, honest, and mutually fulfilling relationships. Healthy caregiving can open the door to a rich intimacy that strengthens a bond of love and friendship, leaving both caregiver and care receiver feeling nourished—as if they've both received a precious gift. Care*taking* might feel like intimacy on the surface, but if you dig deeper, you usually find a false sense of closeness; a distance that can come when one person seeks control over another.

Take a moment to think about the expectations you have for yourself and others. Are they reasonable? Think about moments of disappointment and ask yourself if or how those feelings might be related to unmet or unrealistic expectations. Are lofty or unrealistic expectations negatively affecting your relationships or ability to care*give*?

Sometimes Less Is More

I hope it is clear by now that caring for another being is a *good* thing—a gift that can benefit both the person being cared for and the person doing the caring. I also believe in my heart of hearts that caregiving is an art—an important skill that can be learned, practiced, refined, valued, and shared. Caregiving is a way to develop a stronger and healthier sense of self as we "grow" relationships. Your interest in this book suggests that you are already a caring person. Gaining a better understanding of the differences between care*taking* and care*giving* can help you get the most out of a caring experience. As Melody Beattie wrote, "The most important thing about caretaking is learning to understand what it is and when we are doing it, so we can stop doing it."[3]

Beattie and a host of other experts who have written about codependency and caretaking often talk about a caretaker's tendency to "rescue" instead of being truly helpful. Some experts use the more therapeutic term, describing this habit as "enabling" because it encourages or allows (enables) the care receiver to remain stuck or become helpless and even more dependent on the caretaker. At first the caretaker might feel good, even powerful. But it's often a short trip from rescuer to martyr. Here's what Beattie has to say on the subject:

Rescuing and caretaking mean almost what they sound like. We rescue people from their responsibilities. Later we get mad at them for what we've done. Then we feel used and sorry for ourselves. This is the pattern. . . .

I am not referring to acts of love, kindness, compassion, and true helping—situations where our assistance is legitimately wanted and needed and we want to give that assistance. These acts are the good stuff of life. Rescuing or caretaking isn't.[4]

This kind of caretaking, explains Beattie, requires incompetency on the part of the person being taken care of. "We rescue 'victims'— people who we believe are not capable of being responsible for themselves," she writes.[5] There are, of course, those times when rescuing is necessary and noble. Victims of disasters, people in crisis, those with disabling mental or physical conditions, or babies may truly be helpless and in need of compassionate caregiving.

However, care*takers* often assume someone needs or wants help when they don't. The irony and unintended consequence is that someone the caretaker perceives as helpless who actually is capable can adopt a state of "learned helplessness"—especially if the supposed helpless individual has codependent tendencies of their own. When that happens, there is a risk that both individuals end up feeling lousy because neither is taking care of themselves.

Part of turning care*taking* into care*giving* is learning to sort out what is helping and what is rescuing. As Beattie says, "Most of us truly believe we're helping. Some of us believe we *have to* rescue. We may even think it cruel and heartless to do something as coldblooded as allowing a person to work through or face a legitimate feeling, suffer a consequence, be disappointed by hearing 'no,' be asked to respond to our needs and wants, and generally be held responsible and accountable for him- or herself in this world."[6]

When we jump in to rescue someone who doesn't need rescuing, we may feel more powerful, but we risk taking away that person's power. Even without intending it, we can send the message that we don't think they're capable of taking care of themselves. As Jerry discovered when he moved away from home, it's easy to get used to being looked after by a caretaker.

JERRY'S STORY

I didn't really know how helpless I had become until I moved out of the house and went to college. I love my mom dearly, but she is the classic definition of a caretaker. She anticipated my every need—even when I didn't know I needed something! I didn't learn to budget or balance a checkbook because I didn't have to. I didn't have to be responsible for making sure I had my books or homework or lunch or coat or mittens because she would double-check my backpack each morning when I was little or go over the "checklist" when I was in high school. Don't get me wrong. I'm not blaming her—although some of her babying got a little embarrassing when I got older. I loved being "spoiled" and confess that I still like it when she does my laundry and pampers me when I come home for visits. It was just a rude awakening when I finally got out on my own. But it feels good now knowing that I can do all sorts of things by myself when I need to.

Too often, caretakers live in an "assumptive" world—they assume they know best; they assume they know if someone is in need of help without checking it out or asking if help is wanted; they assume they know how someone feels, how they will act or react.

Care*givers*, on the other hand, learn to check their assumptions at the door. They try not to act impulsively. They *do* try to act with forethought, intention, and respect. As we'll learn in future chapters, this takes patience and practice. But doesn't anything worthwhile?

Caretaking as a Learned Behavior

As Jerry's story demonstrates, our ideas about caring for others and ourselves are usually shaped early on and refined throughout our lives as our social circles and experiences expand. As children, we get clues for how to behave by observing how others behave.

Some of us come from families where we were taught that other people's feelings and needs were more important than our own. Others of us may have had domineering parents who set the bar for excellence so high we thought we were failures if we brought home a "B" instead of the "A" they expected us to achieve. Some of our parents may have done a good job of dividing their time well between family, work, community, and personal concerns. Some of us may have felt ignored by our parents but got positive attention from other caring adults. Others may come from alcoholic or abusive homes where we learned to stifle our feelings and keep the family secrets. Some of us may have an overdeveloped sense of responsibility because of our upbringing; others may often feel helpless because we weren't encouraged to do things on our own.

Whether we heed, reject, or build on the lessons we learn about caring as children depends on our individual inner workings and the external forces and experiences we have encountered as adults. Some of us, like Sheila, were trained to be caretakers but later, under other circumstances, learned to be caregivers.

SHEILA'S STORY

My mother was manipulative and selfish. She brought me up to be her helper because she was "helpless." She stopped working at age fifty-two—six months after I held my first job. Later she developed Alzheimer's. As an only child, I helped her move from public housing to a nursing home, where she died after two years. I took her to doctors; shopped for food, clothes, and medicine; became her guardian; did her books; paid her bills; intervened in crises. She was always mad and verbally abusive throughout this ten-year ordeal. There was nothing rewarding about this time, except once when she said, "You realized how sick I was when I didn't."

My second experience has been very different. My husband was diagnosed with Alzheimer's twelve years ago. He was and is one of the nicest persons on earth, and even though his help-lessness makes a give-and-take relationship virtually impossible, I still love him for what he is inside. But I also feel despair when I see what has happened to him.

What role did you play in your family? What messages were you given about caring for others? What, if any, expectations were communicated to you about how or whether you should care for others? What experiences influence how you think about giving or receiving care? When you think of a caretaker as described in this chapter, who comes to mind? When you think of a caregiver, who comes to mind?

As we shall see, family systems, cultural beliefs and practices, and a variety of experiences all affect how we think, feel, act, and react when it comes to giving and receiving care. Past experiences help shape us, but they needn't hold us hostage. No matter how old or how set in our ways we may think we are, there is always room for change and growth.

CHAPTER 2

Family and Cultural Messages and Expectations about Caregiving

I wish there were shortcuts to wisdom and self-knowledge. . . .
Sadly, it doesn't work that way. I so resent this. The American
way is to not need help, but to help.

—ANNE LAMOTT, *STITCHES: A HANDBOOK ON MEANING, HOPE AND REPAIR*[1]

As Anne Lamott writes in the above excerpt, "The American way is to not need help, but to help." We live in a country of people from different cultures, ethnicities, customs, and beliefs. To understand where and who we are—as caretakers, caregivers, and just human beings in general—I believe it helps to understand where and who we've been. I think looking back can help us move forward.

After identifying some of our own caretaking behaviors in the last chapter, we touched on some of the lessons we learned about caring that helped shape those behaviors. We'll delve a bit deeper into that topic in this chapter. Then we'll look at some ways to counter some of the unhealthy care*taking* messages and integrate more positive care*giving* messages we've received from family, friends, and authority figures—as well as the ones we give ourselves. This is not about "killing the messenger" with blame, rage, guilt, or resentment; it's about understanding the message. It's about being curious and objective enough to use any insights we gain to modify or improve our own caregiving attitudes and behaviors.

Mixed Messages

For many of us, the messages we've gotten over the years about caring and kindness have been mixed, delivered in a "do as I say, not as I do" way that left us doubting the sincerity of the messenger or the value of the lesson. Think of the parent or other adult in a position of authority who preaches the virtue of generosity to a child. They might stress the importance of generosity in one breath, yet complain about "those dirty bums" or "welfare cheats" in the next. Or think of the strict disciplinarian who demands obedience from his children yet brags about the shortcuts he takes at work to avoid responsibility.

As Belinda experienced, the messages we get from our parents about caring for family are often delivered with a degree of expectation that can leave us feeling weighed down by a sense of guilt and responsibility.

BELINDA'S STORY

I fell into caregiving when I was in high school. My dad was chronically ill from a terrible work explosion when he was in his twenties. As a result of terrible burns, his organs were seriously damaged, and high blood pressure was an ongoing problem. I cared for him after school every day. I acted as his nurse. If I had questions, I called my mother at work. If I needed help, I asked a neighbor to come over. He had good and bad days. When he was finally able to go back to work, I moved away to go to college, then got married and had my first child. Dad died after a massive stroke at the age of forty-two.

Many years later, when my mother was dying of cancer, I flew home several times for a week or two to care for her. In her final weeks, I stayed with her until she passed away. During that time, I became so depressed that I asked about hiring around-the-clock nurses. Mom was not happy, and she wrote me a note: "Are you happy spending our money?" She expected me to do what I had done for Dad. I knew she was disappointed that I could not do that again.

Our perspectives on caregiving change as we change. Matthew's story reflects how deeply influenced we are by what we experience and observe growing up and how we are imprinted with the values, fears, desires, strengths, and inadequacies of the adults who cared for us.

MATTHEW'S STORY

My father and I had a long history of conflict. It seemed like we argued about everything. The character of the relationship can have a profound effect upon how care is offered or withheld, and accepted or rejected.

When my mother became seriously ill, my wife and I went to see her. It took no time at all for me to realize that we had walked into a decades old minefield my father and I had created. When I saw that Dad was struggling with the complex regimen of Mom's medications and their restrictions, I set about organizing them. While we were there, the home health care nurse realized that Mom's condition was worsening and urged us to get hospice care. At first Dad resisted, but we insisted and he relented, so my wife worked with the nurse to set that process into motion. Within a few days, we called my siblings and told them Mom was dying and that they should come right away. The changes we made moved Dad off to the sidelines, and he reacted by starting a fight with my wife and me over an issue completely unrelated to Mom's condition. While we three exchanged heated words with each other, Mom was struggling to live out her final days in the adjacent bedroom.

It could have been different, I regretfully realized many years later. When I view the situation through my father's eyes, given our history, I'm sure he saw us less as helpers and more as invaders of his domain. Regardless of our good intentions, I think he felt we emasculated his traditional role as protector and provider for his wife of nearly half a century, and we humiliated his caregiving skills. I think he saw us as trampling over him on our way

*to help Mom. My father died before I had the emotional maturity
to understand the situation from his perspective and apologize for
my part of the conflict.*

Many Definitions of Family

Modern families come in all shapes and sizes—as do the messages
we receive from them. Today, women alone and women together
raise children, just as men alone and men together raise children.
Grandparents and men and women, married and unmarried, raise
children. Many families are "blended" ones, with stepmoms and
stepdads and step- or half-siblings.

Some of us were brought up in families with strong cultural values, beliefs, and traditions that we embraced or rebelled against as
we tested new ideas and tried on new identities.

Others of us had "hippie" parents with a relaxed approach to
child rearing and a peace-and-love ethic that influenced us to pursue
careers in public service. Still others of us may have lived in dys-
functional, destructive, or abusive families that we had to leave to
preserve our sanity. We may have been able to create "new" families
by surrounding ourselves with people who embraced us with genuine love and acceptance and discovered that we could make new
traditions and find the support we missed in our original family. For
many of us, our recovery support group, our religious community, or
a circle of close friends became members of our new family.

I was a single mother during those days of peace, love, long hair,
and bell-bottoms. I worked part time and took classes at the local
university when I could afford them. My friends and I were "hip-
pies," drawn together by the politics and passions of the Vietnam
era. We were more than a tribe or a clan: We were a family. My
daughter and I lived by ourselves, but I always knew that help, support, and companionship were only a phone call away. No one had
much money, so it was common to have community potluck dinners
or picnics. We embraced each other as family and shared child care
responsibilities when we were together.

Although we certainly weren't conscious of it at the time, by operating at this tribal level, we were modeling community for each other and for our children. We abided by unspoken rules of friendship and community that incorporated certain expectations and boundaries. We were comforted and cared for, and we were expected to comfort and care in return.

The point is there is no longer a "one-family-fits-all" formula or ideal, if there ever was.

So when I refer to *family* in this book, know that I am using the term in an inclusive sense to represent not just family of origin or extended family, but those families we have created or discovered.

However we define *family*, each one has its own dynamics—their unique patterns of relating to each other. These patterns vary depending on the structure of the family; the number of children and adults; their relationships, personalities, and cultural backgrounds; and each person's own unique experiences.

Each family also has their own family culture—their unique value systems that can reflect ethnic and cultural backgrounds. These might include beliefs and attitudes about education, gender roles, religion, politics, money, child rearing, medicine and health, food, work and free-time activities, and, of course, kindness and giving help or receiving it from others. A girlhood experience dramatically changed some of the long-held beliefs about self-care that Nora had formed in her family.

NORA'S STORY

I come from a long line of Christian Scientists who believed that prayer—not medicine—was called for when someone got sick. Well, I was on the basketball team in high school, and one day I had a splitting headache. Not knowing my beliefs, a friend put an aspirin in my hand, saying "Take this; you'll feel better." I did, and couldn't believe how much better I felt. It was a miracle! Much to my mother's and grandmother's dismay, that was the day

I knew I could no longer practice their religion—although even now in my eighties, there is a little "cricket" who chirps when I take a pill or go to a doctor!

While family culture can have a profound influence on our caring attitudes and actions, so can events like divorce, trauma, unemployment, poverty, illness, death, or addiction. Always at the ready to give care, Namika found that it was difficult to find herself on the receiving end.

NAMIKA'S STORY

I had a two-week hospitalization in San Francisco and a yearlong recovery after a botched gall bladder surgery that resulted in a damaged pancreas and diabetes. My children were no longer at home, and my husband was very busy with my care, his work, and our home upkeep. My brother and sister-in-law were invaluable, and loving neighbors and friends helped so much too. The greatest gift was that this controlling person—me—learned to receive, sometimes even graciously.

Our definition of *family* can change as our circumstances change. Parents die, children grow up, and they relocate. Part of rebuilding our lives when significant changes occur is deciding whom we want to embrace as family. We can reclaim the word *family* and shape it to fit our life, our relationships, and our reality. Today, I consider my family to be those friends and relatives who share a bond of mutual support and unconditional love—a bond that transcends biology or marriage. They provide a safe place in which to feel and express a range of diverse thoughts and feelings. They are a team that values all members who care for each other in good times *and* bad. William discovered that friends could provide that care when his family was unavailable.

WILLIAM'S STORY

I grew up on the East Coast, and my first job out of college was over one thousand miles away in the Midwest, far away from my family. I was living alone when I got robbed and beaten up very badly, but I had several close friends. One arranged meals to be delivered to me every day, and another friend stopped by all the time just to keep me company. He listened to my fears and never tried to talk me out of feeling what I was feeling. We watched movies and listened to music, and he never got impatient or complained about being bored. I know it was hard, but he hung in there. Just his presence helped me heal. He helped me move forward when it would have been so easy to crawl under a blanket and backslide.

Whom do you include in your family? Who cares for you and whom do you care for? Who keeps you going in times of need or crisis or when you feel stuck? Whom do you support?

Caregiving throughout the Years

Caregiving in today's world differs dramatically from the caregiving in years past. For one thing, we're living longer and moving more. Take my late buddy Emily, for example. Emily was born in 1913 when Woodrow Wilson was president, and she died in 2015 when Barack Obama was president. She was born in Chicago, grew up in Ohio, and then moved to Minneapolis, where she and her husband raised their family. She went back to school after World War II, got her teaching degree, taught school for twenty-one years, worked as a social worker, founded a settlement house, and traveled the world— adventuring in places like Cuba and Turkey or, in her last decades, in the Arctic Circle and an ashram in the mountains to meditate with her granddaughter. At one hundred, although her health was failing, she still volunteered in the schools, played online Scrabble with me (and frequently won), and traveled cross-country to attend her family reunion, where she sunbathed on the North Carolina beaches with her great-grandchildren.

Emily's rich and long life reflects what has happened to many individuals and families in this country as it expanded from a rural to urban then suburban environment and from a predominantly agricultural society to one dominated by industry and technology. Women's roles changed dramatically. Although many poor women have long had to work outside their homes to help provide for their families, in the 1950s and 1960s, most middle-class women did not work at paying jobs outside the home. Today, however, according to the 2014 U.S. Bureau of Labor Statistics, six out of ten women are employed. This means that most family caregivers are employed and trying to balance their work responsibilities with their caregiving duties.[2]

The advent of Social Security in 1935, Medicare and Medicaid in 1965, and the Older Americans Act in 1965 provided more security and services for U.S. citizens in their later years. However, better but more expensive health care has also presented challenges as people with physical and mental health problems live longer and require more of this expensive care. Our society is also more mobile, which means many adult children struggle to arrange care for their elderly parents from a distance. For instance, Emily chose to live in Minneapolis, but she had children on both coasts, and one who lived a few hours away. In addition to their regular visits, they took turns coming to town when a caregiving need arose or communicated with various health care, social service, and transportation agencies via phone or email. Fortunately, Emily's family was able to oversee and be involved in her care until her death at the age of 101, plus she had a vast network of friends and admirers who were always at the ready to help. Unlike too many others, she had the financial means to move to a wonderful assisted living facility in the last few years of her life when she could no longer manage the large family home on her own. Many other families are not as fortunate.

Although the times have indeed changed, many expectations have not, as Lynn Feinberg and Carol Levine explain in their article "Family Caregiving: Looking to the Future":

> Old attitudes persist: families are supposed to take care of older people, without payment or special attention, but policies built upon these assumptions no longer work. Millions of family caregivers today want to take care of their older relatives, but must navigate bewildering and fragmented silos of healthcare and social services.
>
> Caregivers don't know where to turn for help or how to pay for needed services and supports. They often live at a distance from their aging relative, work at a paying job, and must deal with the greater complexity and intensity of caring for someone with multiple chronic conditions and functional impairments. And in the near future, as the population continues to age, these unprecedented challenges will be borne by fewer family caregivers, as people marry later, have fewer (or no) children, divorce and remarry with blended families, and struggle with insecure financial futures.[3]

As they point out, and as I emphasized earlier in this chapter, modern families look and behave much differently than the families of past decades. Individuals of different races, religions, ethnicities, genders, and traditions often join to create something new. Values and traditions may shift or blend, and caregiving expectations may—out of choice or necessity—also change.

Diversity and Caregiving

As many studies on caregiving find, cultural differences often make for different approaches to and attitudes toward caregiving—as do economic, educational, and geographical differences. While most of the articles I've read deal with care of elders, I believe cultural attitudes toward caring for elders can also give us clues to how different communities approach helping in general. For example, many studies have shown that nonwhite caregivers consider caregiving to be less burdensome than white caregivers do, despite the fact that the nonwhite caregiver typically has less income, provides greater amounts of care, and uses fewer professional services.[4]

In African American communities, for example, this decreased sense of burden is usually attributed to a greater tendency to call on friends, neighbors, and church members to help with caregiving tasks. In Latino communities, it is a common expectation that family members will care for an elderly relative. American Indians traditionally hold their elders in very high esteem and want to help them in whatever ways they can because they see this as a way to give back some of what they have been given.[5] While interdependence and support are common in many communities of color, Western Europeans and white ethnic groups appear to place a high value on independence and self-reliance, sometimes making it more stressful to give and accept care.

I suspect that racial oppression and economic disparity also play a role in shaping caregiving attitudes and practices today in this country. In communities where poverty is widespread and government assistance or professional services are difficult to attain, it makes sense that members look to each other for support and help. We certainly witnessed this in African American neighborhoods after Hurricane Katrina.

Jerome was taught early on to turn to a fellow African American community or church member when help was needed.

JEROME'S STORY

I grew up in a pretty poor neighborhood, and things were often hand-to-mouth, especially when my dad wasn't there. He was an over-the-road truck driver, and he'd be gone for long stretches— which was hard on Mom and my six siblings. But we never went hungry. We never had to ask for help; people just knew when a neighbor was hurting. Just when things looked the bleakest, someone from church or the neighborhood would show up at the door with food or clothes or ask us over for a meal. No one ever made a big deal out of it, so we never felt like a charity case. And there was always someone available to watch my little sister or brother if Mom was sick so we older kids didn't have to miss school. When I got a scholarship to go to college, there was a party at the church, and the whole community came out to celebrate. They seemed so proud—like it was one of their own kids! And, in a way, I guess it was.

Studies also reveal that differences and challenges exist for caregivers in rural areas. Poverty and the lack of education, health services, and other resources present particular challenges for those who live away from cities, so family, neighbors, and friends are often called upon to provide both direct and indirect care. However, finding caregivers gets challenging as family members move to pursue job or educational opportunities.

Many lesbian, gay, bisexual, and transgender (LGBT) adults also experience caregiving challenges in their older years. For example, a 2014 study estimated that one in three LGBT older adults lives alone, as compared to one in five non-LGBT older adults. Forty percent of the LGBT older respondents said their support networks became smaller over time, and while LGBT older adults were more likely to face poverty or economic difficulty as they dealt with significant physical or mental health issues, they found that many of the supports in place for the aging in America do not cater to the special needs of LGBT seniors.[6]

While I've witnessed the wonderful closeness and support so apparent in the gay community, many of my lesbian friends without children have expressed concerns about what will happen when they grow old and in need of special care. Here's what Shannon had to say.

SHANNON'S STORY

We breathed easier when the U.S. Supreme Court decided in favor of marriage equality. Even though my partner and I had been together for over twenty years, prior to June 26, 2015, I wasn't entitled to the other benefits heterosexual spouses are entitled to. Now we don't have to worry about my lack of a pension, but we still often wonder what will happen in terms of day-to-day help and emotional support when one of us dies if the other one outlives our close friends. We don't have kids, and our families don't live near us. We're both close to retiring, so we've decided to look for LGBT-friendly senior communities now.

Caregiving attitudes and practices often shift when people move to the United States from other countries and are introduced to American consumerism and lifestyles. As Lian, a Chinese American friend, related in our conversation about heritage, some traditions carry over when parents immigrate to this country, and some cultural caregiving expectations might lessen as adults and children adopt new customs.

LIAN'S STORY

The Chinese culture puts more emphasis on respecting and caring for anyone older than you. That's why children address all adults in your parents' generation as uncles and aunties to show respect. And all adults in your grandparents' generation are called Grandpa and Grandma. As a result, I address our children's nanny as "Auntie," while they call her "Great-Auntie."

Part of this emphasis on respecting and caring for the elderly is even more evident when it comes to your own parents. There's a value called shiou shren, *which has no direct translation in English. But it means you have to obey, care for, and respect your parents. Children are taught that early on. Adult children are obligated to care for their parents physically and financially, and that's why many households have three generations under one roof. Those who can't live with their parents are usually obligated to visit every weekend or live close by for frequent visits. Growing up, every Saturday we visited my dad's parents. Sundays we visited my mom's mom.*

My grandparents all lived with their adult children until they passed. The siblings who didn't live with the parents were very appreciative of the sibling that lived with the grandparents and cared for them daily. And they all made sure to take turns visiting from abroad. The idea of sending your parents to an assisted living or senior living facility was not acceptable and would be very embarrassing for the parents and family members.

I am lucky my parents are open minded and not that traditional about their care when they get older. They talk about planning to live in assisted living communities, and I don't think they expect to live with us. I know they do hope, and most likely expect, that we visit them often—probably every week!

As these statistics and stories indicate, the messages we receive about caring for others are many and varied—and mixed—often leaving us befuddled as we try to sort out what is expected of us and what we expect of ourselves. We are often left wondering what we should or shouldn't do, and when we should or shouldn't do it.

Curbing Our Expectations

If we look again at the stories shared so far in these first chapters, we see that many people talk about or hint at the link between caretaking behaviors and expectations—the expectations perfectionists have for themselves, the expectations that often surround the act of helping and gift giving, or the expectations friends often have of each other. And many of the above stories contain within them the expressed or veiled expectations that parents can have of children, that children frequently have of themselves, or that we create ourselves. Since so many expectations naturally exist in the families and cultures we are born into, I want to spend the rest of this chapter exploring how to deal with the resulting unreasonable expectations that we can carry into our lives as independent adults and what to do with the resentments that often follow.

As was stressed in the first chapter, healthy caregiving isn't about getting rid of all expectations; it's about sorting out reasonable expectations from unreasonable ones. Easier said than done, right? How do we sort out reasonable from unreasonable expectations when so many times our feelings and distorted thinking make sense to *us*?

The first step in letting go of unreasonable expectations is learning how to detect the ones that could lead to disappointment or resentment. For me, it's like sorting through a bag of peaches—which I just did the other day when I was cutting some up for a salad. At first glance, several of them seemed fine. But on closer examination, I discovered some suspicious soft spots and bruises. When I cut those particular peaches open, I was left with a squishy mess that needed to be thrown away. Unmet or unreasonable expectations can leave me feeling the same way—bruised and soft and squishy—so I try to notice when they're creeping into my thoughts.

Whether I think or say them, I find that words like *always* or *never* or *if only* or all the variations of *should*, like *must* or *ought* or *supposed to*, are clues that I'm on my way to forming an unreasonable expectation. On good days, I see the red flags and can interrupt the distorted thought process before the words or expectations take hold. On other days, when I feel disappointed, angry, or resentful, I know that some unreasonable expectations have probably snuck in and escaped the carving knife and garbage. Then I know that they are still with me.

According to many behavioral psychologists, another way to sort out which expectations are realistic and which aren't is to ask if the expectation is helpful or serves us in some way. Some expectations, for instance, might serve as motivators to reach a realistic goal or try something new. Unreasonable expectations are usually pretty rigid.

While we might not be successful in letting go of them entirely, perhaps we can be more flexible and reframe them or let go of a piece of them. For example, while it is unrealistic to expect a friend or family member to give us their total devotion, it is reasonable to expect them to be considerate and respectful. Of course, this also applies to the unrealistic expectations we heap on ourselves when we're operating in full caretaker mode.

I've discovered that another way to check if I may need an "expectation adjustment" is to pay attention to other people's actions and reactions when they express regret about something they've said or done or disappointment or resentment about something someone else has said or done. I try not to slip into my caretaker or "judgey" ways of correcting, controlling, or advising but, instead, try to just listen and learn. So many times, I've had aha moments during exchanges like this, thinking, "Wow, I've felt that very same way—but when I hear him describe his experience, it seems like he's expecting a lot." At times like these, I realize that I'm not looking through a window—I'm often looking in a mirror. Those moments of clarity and connection can help me keep my own expectations in check and—better yet—can help me open myself up to being more understanding of and patient with others. Kayla had a similar experience.

KAYLA'S STORY

When the local car manufacturing plant closed a couple of years ago, a friend of mine who had worked there for over twenty years got laid off. She, of course, was devastated and understandably worried about how she, as a single mom, would be able to make the mortgage, car, and insurance payments, let alone be able to keep helping her two kids in college once her severance pay ran out. I took her out for lunch one day and was surprised at how angry she was at some of her friends and relatives. "I can't believe that I only got calls or cards from a few people," she complained. "I always send or do something if I know someone is sick or going through a hard time. People should know better!"

My first reaction (which I kept to myself) was to think she was being pretty tough on everyone—expecting all her friends to know what she was going through. Then I stopped to think of how I felt when I was going through a hard time. I remembered having some of those same expectations. Plus, sometimes I think you don't know where to direct your feelings, and they come out sort of sideways. I don't think some of her friends even knew what had happened. Even if they did, I know some people don't know what to say—it's scary for all of us to think how fast the rug can be pulled out from under us. But I didn't make excuses or try to talk her out of her feelings. It was a lousy turn of events, and I think she just needed to vent.

As Kayla and I both discovered, realizing that other people have similar expectations can help us "normalize" our own feelings when we have unmet expectations about our own or someone else's behavior. And that realization often makes it easier to soften or let those expectations go.

Some dictionaries explain that the word *expectation* comes from the Latin word for "awaiting." Thinking of an expectation in this way reminds me of the best piece of advice a therapist once gave me when I expressed hurt and disappointment over something that had happened in a close relationship. "Be curious," she urged me. "Try not to enter situations with preconceived notions of what will or should happen. Try to relax a little and let things just unfold as they will. Who knows—you might be delightfully surprised."

I can't tell you how often her words of wisdom float back to me, lessening my fear, my anxiety, and—yes, you guessed it—my expectations. When we were talking about this subject, a friend reminded me of how Buddhists approach the idea of expectations. "They teach the importance of freeing ourselves from expectations that can control us and distort our reality, and not getting attached to outcomes," he said.

Author Phillip Moffitt talks more about this at his website, Dharma Wisdom. He stresses how normal it is to have expectations, but cautions that when we allow them to rule our lives, we risk closing ourselves off to possibilities and the present wonder of each moment—which is just what my therapist was hinting at.

> What is most amazing is that despite the suffering caused by your expectations, you hardly notice them most of the time. Sure, there may be a few big ones you are somewhat aware of, but even so, you only sort of notice them; you do not act to free yourself from their tyranny. Plus, there are countless smaller ones you never notice at all. It is only when you feel acute disappointment that you have any awareness of having been possessed by expectations. . . .
>
> . . . As you learn to free yourself from these larger expectations, you can start to notice the smaller ones and not allow them to define your daily experience. You may expect that certain efforts will yield desired results, or believe you can be in control of your life, or be totally convinced that the so-called good life must have particular components. You may be enslaved by your expectations of what defines a good marriage, a good person, or success. More than likely, you expect to behave in a manner you know is right, and you expect to be treated similarly. Left unnoticed, these expectations become all-powerful. Just think of the amount of suffering—yours and the suffering of others—that comes from these unrecognized expectations; it is a call for mindfulness and for choosing not to be defined by expectations.[7]

We'll talk more about mindfulness when we talk about self-care in later chapters, but for now I urge you to think about your own expectations—the ones you have for yourself and the ones you have for others. If it helps, you may want to brainstorm a list of these. Are your expectations reasonable? Which ones frequently go unmet? What happens when you don't get the result or reaction you expect? Is there a way to lessen, let go of, or reframe your expectations? How do you think it would feel to be more curious and open yourself to possibility instead of having preconceived notions of what should or should not be?

Releasing Resentments

It is natural to feel a bit let down when we do something nice for someone and get no sign of acceptance in return—not even a quiet thank-you, a smile, or a hug of gratitude. If we let the disappointment build, however, it can turn into an all-out grudge—a sign that we are leaning a little to the care*taker* side of our caretaker/caregiver chart. That's when we realize the truth of that saying from the last chapter about how expectations can turn into resentments.

In Latin, the word *resent* means "to feel again." Resentment is unresolved anger that can slow our progress from caretaker to caregiver. When we feel resentful, we often replay a scene over and over again until it takes on a life of its own. When this happens, it's easy for other scenes, omissions, or wrongs that have been done to us by that person or others to pile on and grow, leaving us feeling self-righteous, deflated, hurt, or even hate-filled. I find that can be when those loaded words of expectation creep into my head: "This *always* happens; he *never* . . ."

I believe that, once planted, the seeds of resentment have the ability to grow into an overall bitterness that can negatively affect the way we act toward or give care to others. What's that saying about "once bitten, twice shy"? If memory serves, it originally referred to dog bites, but I think it could apply to caregiving just as well. If a caring act backfires, we might get a bad taste in our mouth about doing future favors—at least for that person.

Here's my own story of how that can happen. I wrapped myself in anger and bitterness toward my father-in-law for years, even after he died. The two of us were like oil and water—we just didn't mix. I know I didn't match the picture he had of what his son's wife should be like. He was a devout Catholic, and I came from a family of Protestants. I was a divorcee with a child. I hated his politics, and he disapproved of my feminism. But I loved his son deeply, so I put on my best care*taker* hat and tried for decades to get my husband's father to love me too.

I could have scored 100 percent on the caretaker chart. I needed to be needed; I wanted to be special in his life; I offered false praise, tried to please him and win him over. I baked cookies, gave unwanted gifts. For god's sake, I sewed him a bathrobe he didn't need or want! My "selfless" gestures were usually met with indifference or a little suspicion. Of course they were, because they weren't genuine. My ulterior motives were showing. But I didn't realize that at the time.

Instead, I harbored a grudge beyond all grudges. Although perhaps justified because he truly did not treat me very nicely, my resentment grew. Someone said that hanging on to resentment is like letting someone live rent-free in your head. I allowed my father-in-law to be a squatter in my brain for more than a quarter of a century. The more I obsessed and judged and wallowed in self-pity, the more power he had over me.

It wasn't until he was dying that I started to release the resentment that had held *me* captive all those many years. I stood by my husband's side at his father's hospital bed, looking down at this old, small, and vulnerable man, now lying in quiet pre-death stillness. The bitterness that had so weighed me down for so long began to lift.

It took more time, more honest self-reflection, and more maturity, but some years later, I was finally able to let go of the toxic resentment I had carried for way too long. At long last, I realized that my "righteous" anger was turning me into someone I didn't like all that much when I fumed to myself or to others about all the injustices I had suffered, whether real or imagined. I had allowed all sorts of negative feelings to get in my way, preventing me from connecting with the better parts of myself that hold love, compassion, and joy.

This abandonment of rage is, for me, forgiveness. It isn't cheap "I'm sorrys" that are delivered too quickly or casually, and it doesn't require participation or even knowledge from the other person. It can be an independent—even revolutionary—act of self with and for self. This style of forgiveness can share a bed with anger, just as joy can live with grief.

Booker T. Washington said, "I shall allow no man to belittle my soul by making me hate him." If an emancipated slave can be that generous, I figure I should be able to let go of some of my dark emotions. I spent way too much time and way too much energy resenting my father-in-law. Now that I've canceled his "squatter's rights," he no longer lives "rent-free in my head." I've forgiven him—or perhaps it's myself that I have forgiven.

I regret that self-awareness took so long, however, and I can't help but wonder what our relationship could have been like if I had been less the needy care*taker* and more the compassionate care*giver* while he was alive.

Defusing Resentments

When we "defuse" something, we disarm it—like a munitions expert would disconnect the wires on a bomb to keep it from exploding. When we defuse resentments, we usually find they lose their power. One way to get resentments out of our heads is to write them down. When we see them on our computer screen or on a piece of paper, we often discover they seem different—perhaps less reasonable than we thought at first. Some of them might even look silly once we see them in black and white. Those in Twelve Step groups would call this doing an "inventory," an exercise that can benefit everyone—not just those in recovery from addiction.

Hazelden Publishing's book *Recovery Now* likens a personal inventory to a business inventory, "where a business owner sorts through products to see which are usable, which are damaged, and which can't be sold." It goes on to say:

> When we take our own personal inventory, we list our character traits, behaviors, and distorted thoughts and feelings that feed our addictive behavior. We also take note of our positive

traits and moral principles, which may have been hidden during our active addiction. These are things that can help us in recovery. In addition, we list the people who may have been harmed by our addictive behavior—including ourselves. . . . A business that tries to sell damaged goods goes broke. An addicted person who clings to damaged thoughts and feelings also goes "broke."[8]

If we substitute *caretaker* for *addicted person* in the last sentence of the above excerpt, we can see how worthwhile writing down our resentments could be. Resentments can grow out of unresolved anger and a belief that we have been wronged in some way (which was the case in my relationship with my father-in-law). As I discovered, holding on to these feelings can rob us of our ability to feel compassion or give care with no strings attached.

Ben was like many people who shared their stories with me and who spoke of how hard it is for them to now show concern and care for elderly parents who had mistreated or abandoned them and their siblings when they were children and needed them the most.

BEN'S STORY

My dad was an alcoholic who walked out when I was a freshman in high school and my brother and sister were in junior high and middle school. My mother was so lost and depressed that she couldn't really take care of us, let alone herself. Plus, by that time, her own drinking was getting out of control. I was oldest, and I tried to make sure we got to school, and the three of us did our best to take care of her and the house. Sometimes a neighbor or out-of-town relative would show up with a little money or some food or clothes, but it was embarrassing to know that kids looked down at us. We were poor, and we looked like it. Then one day she just took off with a guy she met at a bar. The neighbors must have contacted the authorities, and we got taken to our grand-parents' house—which was no picnic. She came back after about six months, filled with promises and apologies, but things were always unstable, and we never knew when or if she'd be around.

Fast-forward thirty years to present time. My mother isn't drinking anymore, but the years of hard living, alcohol, and pills have taken their toll, and she is in very poor health. My siblings moved away years ago, and I feel responsible—like I'm a kid again. She lives in public housing, and her Social Security checks don't go very far, so I try to help out when I can. Plus my brother and sister will chip in once in a while too. But her frequent calls expecting my wife or me to take her to a doctor or to a store, fix her TV, balance her checkbook, or invite her over to our house are stressing me out and driving me crazy.

As many of us may have already found, anger is not usually the problem. Anger is a normal, often useful emotion that can motivate us to make necessary changes. It's holding on to anger until it turns into resentment that can make us miserable. We can't control what others do or change what they did. But we can control how we respond.

When we do a resentment inventory, we write down a list of people we resent and describe what happened and how we feel about it. Then it is useful to write down how holding on to the resentment is harming us. Is it keeping us from trusting? Is it causing rage or sadness or depression? Is it affecting our self-esteem, our ambition, or our other relationships?

The last step in this process is to brainstorm ways we might lessen or let go of each resentment. Ben's wife came from a close family who genuinely cared about each other, so he had been hesitant to share his feelings with her. Ben's wife hadn't known his mother at her worst, so he worried that she might not understand his feelings or might think he was being unkind or selfish when he wasn't all that keen about helping her. When his stress and depression began to affect their marriage, however, he opened up and, together, he and his wife came up with some strategies to lessen his caretaking burden. They found some community resources like Meals on Wheels and a van service that could take his mother shopping, to the doctor, or to church, and they asked for more help from the other siblings.

As Ben felt his responsibilities lift, he also experienced less resentment and anger and blame toward his mother. He said that some days he is even able to look at his mother's life more objectively and admit that she had it pretty rough herself, being left alone with three kids and no money. He said she seems to be making an effort now to be kinder and more appreciative. She enjoys seeing her grandkids, and Ben said they've actually had some pleasant outings as a family. He has no delusions that theirs will ever be a perfect mother/son relationship, but he said he is more willing and less bitter about helping her since his "attitude adjustment."

Some members of our caregivers' group came up with a ritual to let go of some of the undesirable feelings we experienced in conjunction with our caregiving duties. We met at a member's house, and, after taking some time to talk about the negative feelings that often arose, we were each given a piece of paper. During fifteen minutes of silence, we each made our individual list of uncomfortable or unwanted feelings like resentment, self-pity, martyrdom, anger, loneliness, neediness, regret, blame, guilt, or impatience. Those who wanted to read their lists out loud did so; others preferred to keep theirs to themselves. Then each of us took turns putting our list in the fire in the fireplace. Seeing those unwanted, often unhealthy feelings go up in flame was a powerful experience.

After the burning, we were given another piece of paper on which we listed the things we envisioned replacing those feelings we released. Yesterday, I found my list of desired qualities tucked away in a book of poetry: "compassion, acceptance, desire to risk and create, joy of discovery, possibility, generosity of spirit, understanding, laughter, grace and gratitude, trust in myself and in others, self-worth, healthy boundaries, confidence, tolerance, and patience." Although I didn't realize it until this moment, many of the items on those lists ended up in the chart of caretaker/caregiver characteristics I created in chapter 1.

What caretaker feelings would you list that you want to get rid of? What qualities would you like to replace them with?

The Road from Resentment to Forgiveness

Someone wrote that forgiveness is giving up the idea that we could have had a different past. When we lessen the grip we have on resentment—and the stranglehold it has on us—we pave the way to the sort of forgiveness that frees us to live life more fully in the present moment. This type of forgiveness is *not* forgetting, excusing, or reconciling (although, of course, it might eventually lead to reconciliation). As Ben discovered, he could choose to forgive his mother, yet still be mad at her for neglecting her children.

Healthy forgiveness is not the simple or hasty "I'm sorry" we were taught to say whenever our parents demanded that response. Real forgiveness is hard and contemplative work that we practice one day and one experience at a time. It is a path to our healing that begins and ends with compassion for ourselves and our feelings, a path that can lead from unhealthy care*taking* to more fulfilling care*giving*. Perhaps rather than "forgive and forget," our new motto should become "forgive and live."

In the next chapter, we'll discuss the importance of establishing and maintaining healthy and respectful boundaries in all our caregiving interactions, big and small, and how such a practice can work as a "resentment prevention tool."

CHAPTER 3

Balance and Boundaries

*Perhaps I'll define my boundaries with Post-it Notes
instead of police tape.*
—MISTI B., *IF YOU LEAVE ME, CAN I COME WITH YOU?*[1]

By now I'm hoping you have a clearer picture of the differences between care*taking* and care*giving* and a better understanding of how the messages we receive from childhood onward can influence how we respond to those who are in need or want of care. Some of the people we've heard from in the first chapters described caring relationships that are close and respectful. Some talked about the tension and conflict they experienced in their families of origin. Others spoke of the pressure or expectation that often comes with giving care.

The way we relate to others has a lot to do with the kinds of boundaries we establish and maintain with them. A boundary is an invisible line that separates what we are responsible for from what others are responsible for. Appropriate boundaries can protect and preserve our individuality and help keep our self-esteem intact. Unfortunately, boundaries are often the first things to go when it comes to giving or receiving care.

Boundary setting can be particularly difficult when we slip into care*taker* mode. Caretakers tend to function at extremes. They might operate with few (or no) boundaries and might do things like open themselves up to people they hardly know or get overinvolved in a friend's or loved one's life and problems when it is not their place to do so. At the other extreme, they might build walls and operate with rigid boundaries if they feel wronged or unappreciated for all the sacrifices and efforts they have made when giving care—even if their care wasn't asked for or wanted. In the language of codependency, you might say that care*takers* have a hard time figuring out where they end and others begin.

Enmeshed or Disengaged?

As is the case with so many other things, most of us learn about boundaries early in our lives. Salvador Minuchin, a pioneer in the field of structural family therapy, was one of the first to describe a family with no boundaries or blurred boundaries as an "enmeshed" family system. He called families with rigid boundaries "disengaged."[2] Enmeshed family systems tend to produce people who think fuzzy boundaries are normal, and they behave accordingly. Disengaged family systems tend to produce people who think isolation is normal, and they behave accordingly.

Minuchin wrote that we travel on a continuum from disengagement to enmeshment that looks like this:

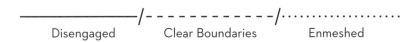

Disengaged　　　　Clear Boundaries　　　　Enmeshed

Being enmeshed or disengaged is a habit of thought and behavior. Care*taking* habits usually seem normal until they are challenged, and we discover we have choices and new options. As we get more in tune to the reactions of others and pay closer attention to our own actions and reactions, we become more aware of where we are on the disengaged/enmeshed continuum. We practice setting and maintaining boundaries with the goal of operating more in the middle ground of healthy caregiving whenever possible. As we do this, we discover which behavior and boundary feels most appropriate. Ideally, we can practice boundary setting without succumbing to anger, shame, regret, or embarrassment. With practice, we can get better at identifying and respecting our own and other people's boundaries.

So often the line from the James Taylor song "Shed a Little Light" comes to mind when I've crossed someone's boundary or when someone has crossed one of mine—it is the feeling "like the clenching of a fist." Sometimes I don't have that feeling right away; it's something that builds, often after I've obsessed about an awkward interaction or a troubling event. Sometimes I actually wake up with my fists clenched—a dead giveaway that there's been a boundary violation.

Of course it's normal to slide along the continuum. As has been emphasized several times already, caring for others is a fluid activity with different "rules" for different situations. In times of crisis or serious illness, it might be necessary to become somewhat enmeshed when caring for a loved one or to "disengage" (temporarily or permanently) from an unhealthy relationship that is interfering with our ability to give appropriate care to our loved one or to ourselves.

Lou shared how as he moved from childhood to adulthood, he moved from enmeshment to disengagement in his relationship with his parents. This allowed him to be a healthier caregiver when he married and had a family of his own.

LOU'S STORY

I didn't think I had a choice when it came to taking care of my parents. One time, before I was married, I got a last-minute call to pick up my dad, who was getting released from yet another detox facility—this one out of state. My mother refused to get him, so I thought that meant I had to, even though I had tickets to go to a concert with my girlfriend and another couple. It took over six hours to get him and deliver him to his place. Then I had to turn around and pick up my date and friends and drive over an hour to the concert. I was so tired at the end of the night that I came very close to falling asleep at the wheel. That moment still haunts me, thinking about how I could have killed us all.

Years later, I was married and my wife was in labor with our first baby. My father called yet again, needing to be rescued. At that point, I told him I now had other responsibilities and he had to find his own way. This was a small but important step toward establishing healthier boundaries.

From where on the disengagement/enmeshment continuum do you think you usually operate? Can you think of times when you've operated at either or both extremes? How about those times when you've maintained healthy boundaries by operating in the middle ground? Do you think your boundaries are too weak, too strong, or just right?

Different Types of Boundaries

Simply put, when we set boundaries, we set limits. When we practice healthy boundary setting, we learn there are times we like to be close, and there are times we need to be alone. We also learn that we have the right to say no if our rights are violated or space is invaded. Although it's difficult, care*takers* on their way to care*giving* discover that having the courage to set boundaries, even when doing so risks disappointing someone, is about self-awareness and self-respect. Healthy boundaries allow us to express and show concern without rescuing, enabling, controlling, or fixing someone or something.

There are several different types of boundaries, and how we honor another person's boundaries or maintain our own depends on the person and the circumstances.

Physical Boundaries

Physical boundaries have to do with personal space, privacy, and bodies. Unless we are pulling someone out of harm's way or rescuing their belongings from a fire, we don't have the right to touch other people or their things without permission, just as they don't have the right to touch us or our things without our permission. Those who practice good boundary setting don't assume someone—adult or child—is comfortable hugging, for example. If you don't know for certain if someone is a "hugger," it's fine to check this out by asking, "Is it okay to hug you?" I've found that people who do not choose to embrace those they do not know all that well or who just don't like to hug are usually good at communicating that preference through their body language by stepping back a little or extending their hand in a handshake or wave when a conversation or interaction has ended.

Another way to honor someone's physical boundaries is to respect their privacy by not dropping by unexpectedly at their home, their workplace, or their hospital room without contacting them or their primary caregiver first. I've gotten better about setting my own boundaries in this regard because I work out of my home and know how disruptive an unexpected visit can be. I often wake up with a thought I want to get down on paper and then lose myself in my writing well after my breakfast and first cup of coffee. It's embarrassing to have the doorbell ring at 11:00 a.m. when I'm still in my pajamas!

MICHELLE'S STORY

I never thought much about dropping in on someone or having them drop in on me until my mom grew old and had more physical problems. She lives alone, and it is very difficult for her to get to the door—plus there was a break-in in the neighborhood, so she is a little afraid to answer the door if she is not expecting someone. She loves visitors, but I worry about her.

*Her church has a volunteer care team who visit the elderly,
and they're great about calling ahead or having a certain day and
time each week when they stop by so she won't be surprised. She
loves to look her best for the visits so she has time to get herself
and the house ready. I also put a "no solicitations" sign on her
door, so that's kept the "door knockers" away. Mom's experience
has made me more sensitive about this whole issue, and I try now
to always call first before I stop by anyone's house—even my best
friend's.*

Emotional Boundaries

Emotional boundaries separate our emotions (and responsibility
for them) from another person's. When we maintain appropriate
emotional boundaries, we learn to put the brakes on before we offer
advice, blame someone for our actions or reactions, or accept the
blame for their actions or reactions. Healthy emotional boundaries
can protect us from feeling responsible for another's problems or
from taking their negative comments personally if we have done
nothing to warrant them.

When we practice good emotional boundaries, we get more
in tune with which interactions are helpful and which might be
hurtful. We can step back and accept the feelings of others without
thinking we need to fix them or solve their problems. And we get
better at accepting our own feelings without thinking something is
wrong with us that needs to be fixed.

We also get better at knowing when and whether intimacy is
appropriate—when it's okay to confide or share personal feelings or
experiences, and when or whether it feels appropriate for someone
else to be sharing theirs with us. Without even knowing why or
how it happens, care*takers* frequently have strangers or acquaintances share things that would normally be told to a close friend
or therapist. Care*givers* try to remember that they are there to listen, support, empower, and offer help that is within bounds—and
boundaries.

JOHN'S STORY

I always thought I was a good listener until my teenage son exploded one day out of total frustration, saying, "Dad, you never just listen! I don't need you to solve all my problems; I just wanted to tell you about what was going on at school." This really got to me and caused me to do some honest soul searching. I realized I do this a lot—with friends, with my wife, with my kids. . . . I want to let myself off the hook by saying it's just a guy thing, but I've noticed a lot of women friends doing it too.

I was talking to my wife about this, and she dug up a handout about listening she had gotten at a class she went to years ago. I made a copy and keep it by my bedside as a reminder to pay closer attention to people and to try to keep my mind from racing ahead trying to think of the solution or best response.

I've included the piece John is referring to below (and I've shared it in other books I've written) because I think it so clearly addresses a common caretaker characteristic. It might be familiar to you since it's been out there for years. I keep my own well-worn copy close at hand as a good boundary reminder.

Could You Just Listen?

When I ask you to listen to me, and you start giving me advice, you have not done what I asked.

When I ask you to listen to me, and you begin to tell me why I shouldn't feel that way, I feel like you are ignoring my feelings.

When I ask you to listen to me, and you feel you have to do something to solve my problem, I often get more confused, strange as that may seem.

All I ask is that you listen, not talk or do—just hear me.

When you accept as a simple fact that I do feel what I feel, no matter how irrational, then I can quit trying to convince you and can get about the business of understanding what's behind this feeling.

So, please listen and just hear me.

And if you want to talk, wait a minute for your turn—and I'll listen to you.

—Author unknown (adapted)

Mental Boundaries

Mental boundaries have to do with how we and others see the world—how we think about things like politics, the environment, career choices, child rearing, education, family, friendships, and caregiving. Care*takers* can have difficulty expressing their beliefs or opinions because they may feel intimidated by someone else's knowledge, or they are easily persuaded to accept another person's point of view in order to keep the peace or avoid conflict. They might also have difficulty listening with an open mind to someone else's beliefs or opinions.

And because they often want to feel in control, care*takers* may also find it difficult to hold their tongues if they disagree with someone's choices. While care*givers* might offer resources and information if asked to do so, they try not to interfere with someone's plan of action, whether that plan has to do with health concerns or home improvements—even though they may strongly disagree. They try not to be "know-it-alls," and unless asked, "What do you think?" they try to keep their differing opinions to themselves. Roberta has struggled with keeping her mental boundaries since childhood.

ROBERTA'S STORY

We always joke that being right in my family was a contact sport. It didn't matter what the subject was—politics, religion, science—one person would express an opinion or relate something that had happened or was in the news, and another person would jump in to disagree or challenge whatever had been said.

That habit has carried over into my adulthood, and I have to constantly watch myself in a group of people because I automatically want to debate. I know from their reactions what a turnoff that can be.

Spiritual Boundaries

The Franciscan friars have a saying: "I don't want a God who is reduced to the limits of my imagination." I have long been of the opinion that spirituality is an ever-evolving, fluid stirring within us that is different for each individual. Some might connect spirituality with the God of traditional religions; others might refer to their Higher Power, which they could define as nature or a support group. Some might describe spirituality as the thread that connects us from self to others.

When we practice healthy spiritual boundaries, we accept that there are many paths to a source of higher meaning or purpose. When we are being our best caregiver selves, whether doing a favor or sitting at a loved one's deathbed, we realize it is not our job to foist our beliefs on them or challenge theirs, any more than we would want them to force theirs on us. It is not our job to convince them of God, or of heaven, hell, or some other religious concept. Caregivers provide comfort and help and companionship. They can call the person's spiritual advisor if the person requests such a visit—but they don't assume that role themselves.

A healthy caregiver/care receiver relationship is one in which boundaries are not only strong, they're pliable enough to bend as situations and people change. Here again, self-awareness comes to play when defining and recognizing appropriate boundaries and setting and maintaining our own. Dana made this discovery with a friend whose spiritual path was unfamiliar and made her uncomfortable at first.

DANA'S STORY

I've learned so much about boundary negotiation from my friend who joined a Sufi (the mystical branch of Islam) community years ago. Quite honestly, it weirded me out when this happened, and our friendship felt a little awkward because I didn't understand her choices. She sensed this and took the first step by saying, "You've seemed a little uncomfortable lately. Is there anything you want to ask me?"

We spent two hours talking about her journey, and she was so open to any questions I had about Sufism and how it compared and contrasted with other major religions. She didn't "preach," and I never felt like she was trying to convince me of anything. And I didn't argue or try to convince her. We found points of connection, and our friendship got back on track.

What are your physical, emotional, mental, and spiritual boundaries? How do you know or feel when someone crosses one of your boundaries? Have you inappropriately crossed a boundary by trying to "fix" a situation or person, trying to take charge when it was not your place to do so, or going overboard when offering your time or money when providing care?

Setting Boundaries

Setting boundaries is about acknowledging limits, not building walls. The goal is to gain enough sense of self and of others that we can get comfortably close to other people without disappearing in their shadows or taking over their lives. When our boundaries are unclear, it is often too easy to get pulled into someone's pain and problems or give too much because we've lost sight of our own needs or limitations.

Caretakers often have trouble setting boundaries because they get used to putting other people's needs before their own, or they might worry that setting a boundary could threaten a relationship.

Like most worthwhile endeavors, boundary setting takes practice. But setting and sticking to boundaries can help us decide if, when, and to whom we choose to give care.

To begin with, it is important to try to set boundaries when the air is calm and clear—when we aren't tired, angry, hurt, resentful, or in the midst of a crisis. While we can have different boundaries for different situations and relationships, let's explore some of the things we can do to recognize and set appropriate boundaries with each caring opportunity.

Evaluating the Need

Determining how great or immediate a need is can help us decide if or how much help is called for and how much we are willing to invest in helping. Is this a onetime favor? Will this person require ongoing care on a daily, weekly, or monthly basis? Are there others who will also be involved in helping this person? Unless it is a true emergency, taking time to objectively evaluate a situation before rushing forward to offer our help is an important step in boundary setting. Without boundaries, what starts out as an occasional offer of help can easily turn into an ongoing and often overwhelming responsibility.

Needs can change, of course, but so can boundaries. Setting boundaries helps caregivers sort out their needs from those of the person they are helping. If we agree to do one small favor but then get that clenched-fist feeling because we're expected to be more servant than helper, it's time to go back to the boundary drawing board. When we honor our own boundaries, we give ourselves permission to change our initial yes to a yes with conditions (e.g., I can help you with your bills once a month; I can take you to the doctor for your bimonthly checkup; I can watch your kids every other week to give you a break). Or we might realize we've been stretched beyond our limits, and we need to turn the responsibility over to someone else. Sometimes saying yes to ourselves means saying no to others.

Understanding Our Motivations

At those times when we have the luxury of choosing to offer a helping hand (versus assuming the role of primary caregiver because of an illness or crisis), it's important that we do so with intention and self-awareness. Here again, it helps to pause and take time to do some honest self-reflection before volunteering our time or services.

If you are unclear of your motivations, it might be helpful to check in with yourself by reviewing the caretaker/caregiver chart in chapter 1 (see pages 16–18 and appendix C). If your desire to help has more to do with your needs than the other person's, the care relationship risks getting out of balance, and then boundaries can quickly get blurred.

Balance and Commitment

Before we take on a caring responsibility—no matter how big or how little—it's important to have a good idea of what other areas of our lives will be affected. Figuring out as closely as we can how much time will be involved will give us a clue if we will still have enough time for other priorities like family, friends, work, exercise, and sleep. It is common for caretakers to overcommit to others and undercommit to themselves. Establishing healthy boundaries—that invisible line between self and others—can help us keep things in better balance. A balanced care relationship is one that doesn't overpower or deplete either party.

Balance, like limits, depends on one's own perspective and experiences. For example, I was one of the principal caregivers for my mom when she was diagnosed with cancer. Shortly before she died—on one of those fifteen-hour days by her hospital bedside—she took my hand and looked at me, saying, "I don't know what I'd do without you." Because we enjoyed a wonderful relationship at that point in our lives, I was able to hear her words as an expression of love and gratitude. I chose to be there; I needed to be by her side, so nothing seemed out of balance. However, for others who may have grown up in abusive households or for those who might be in a difficult relationship with a relative or friend, being called upon to help them may seem (understandably) like a heavy weight they carry out of obligation, not choice. For them, my mother's words could be interpreted as pressure, even manipulation. For them, the message might mean, "I *expect* your selfless devotion." For them, the whole situation may seem out of balance.

Reality Check

Remember what was said about caretakers often wanting to be the "special one"? Helping someone can boost our self-esteem and confidence—especially if the task at hand is one that we're especially suited for. But what about those times when what is called for doesn't match our knowledge or abilities all that well?

An honest assessment of our capabilities is another way to set a boundary. If we acknowledge our limits and admit we aren't the best person for the job, we can still support and help by figuring out who might be better able to do what is needed. Acknowledging our limitations before we find ourselves over our heads is a good exercise in both boundary setting *and* caregiving. Instead of always wanting to be managers, we practice being helpful assistants.

Prepare Yourself for Setting Boundaries

When caregivers feel especially fragile—when they're low on energy and high on emotions, feeling anxious and overwhelmed or ready to cry or explode—it's a good clue they need to set or adjust a boundary. It's never too late to set a boundary, but having them in place ahead of time can help us pull back a bit *before* things get out of control or we become totally exhausted. Boundaries are like firm taps on the shoulder that remind us to pause before we overcommit, say or do something inappropriate, or allow someone to disrespect or take advantage of us.

One way to help get boundaries in place is to do a little brainstorming by listing our rights and preferences. Take a digital or paper sheet and try completing the following sentences by writing down as many things as you can think of:

I have the right to _____ .
(For example, my own space; ask for support; say no; my own feelings; choose the kind of help I want to offer; change doctors or get a second opinion; decide what I am responsible for; decide what I want to share and with whom)

People may not _____ .
(For example, criticize or humiliate me in front of others; invade my personal space or belongings; emotionally or physically abuse me)

To protect my time and energy, it's okay to _____ .
(For example, change my mind; not answer the phone; say no; establish healthy priorities; say "let me think about it" before I agree to something)

When setting boundaries with others, it's important not to get defensive or overexplain because it's easy for them to then focus on the explanation and lose sight of the boundary request. And once a boundary is established, it's also important to back it up with action. If we don't honor our own boundaries, we invite others to ignore them too.

Here are some examples of how you might set boundaries with another person. Can you think of others?

- My family has a rule about no phone calls during meals, and we're eating right now, so I'll have to call you back.

- I really want to help you on moving day, but I'll have to check my schedule and get back to you.

- I have really enjoyed being a member of Jo's care team, but there are some family matters that need my attention right now, so I'm going to have to take a break after this week.

- It's always great to see you, but could you call before you stop by next time to be sure I'm home and not working?
- Wednesday mornings don't work for me because I have a fitness class that day. Could we schedule a different time?
- I'm not really comfortable talking about Madeline and Jack's situation; I think you should call them directly.

Try to have fun doing these exercises by coming up with other situations that can frustrate or annoy you (especially caregiving situations). Think of how you might respond next time they occur—because there almost always is a next time! Are you usually the go-to person for friends and family for house or car maintenance, errands, child care, or other such tasks? Does someone frequently keep you on the phone for over an hour even though you've said "I have to get going" or "I've only got a minute" at the beginning of the conversation? Is there a friend or relative who often asks for monetary loans or other favors? If these are areas of irritation, how might you establish a better boundary?

Change What You Can Change

Viktor Frankl, a psychiatrist who was imprisoned in a Nazi concentration camp during World War II, wrote how that experience taught him that everything can be taken from us except one thing, which he described as "the last of human freedoms—to choose one's own attitude in any given set of circumstances, to choose one's own way."[3] Setting boundaries and respecting the boundaries of others helps us choose and sort out which attitudes, behaviors, or practices work well; which we want to discard; and which ones may need adjusting.

Some people find that the Serenity Prayer that Alcoholics Anonymous (AA) has embraced since the organization discovered it in 1948 helps in the process of making and practicing boundaries.

God, grant me the serenity
to accept the things I cannot change,
courage to change the things I can,
and wisdom to know the difference.

There are several versions of this prayer, and it has been variously attributed to an ancient Sanskrit text, to Aristotle, to St. Augustine, to St. Francis of Assisi, and to others. (AA generally credits the version they use to theologian Reinhold Niebuhr.) You don't have to be religious to recite this prayer; you don't even have to believe in a god—just start the prayer with "Grant me the serenity . . ." if that is the case.

In terms of boundary keeping, the things we cannot change might be the people or circumstances that are causing us distress. The things we can change could be our own actions, reactions, views, or the things we can put up with. The wisdom to know the difference between what we can change and cannot change comes with practice. Even though practice doesn't always "make perfect," it can sharpen our awareness of when we screw up. Take me, for example.

I've been using the Serenity Prayer as a mantra for many decades, yet I still catch myself trying to change what I should know by now I cannot change—like last summer when my husband and I went to a lovely little river town for a few days with three other couples. We've all been close friends for around forty years, and we have supported each other in joyous times and in difficult times. We are quick to applaud individual successes and aware of each other's strengths and shortcomings. Thank goodness we are also quick to forgive, because I felt I needed it on this particular trip.

Here's what happened:

I've known and loved our friend Rob since before he married my close friend and long-ago roommate, Laura. But even after all these many years, he can still drive me crazy because he doesn't act or react the way *I* think he should. On last summer's trip, each couple took a turn with meal and kitchen tasks, and on Laura and Rob's night, I grew irritated, then furious, when Rob sat outside with us while Laura cooked and got things ready. She had recently had some health problems, so I was admittedly overprotective of her that night. I tried shaming him with "I thought it was *your* turn to help too." When one of the other guys got up to help her in the kitchen, I tried manipulation. "Well, it looks like he's doing *your* job." But all I got in return from Rob was a nonchalant shrug and, "I'd just be in the way." All of us have long known that in their house, Laura has always been responsible for household things while Rob has always taken care of the garden and other outdoor jobs, yet I was on this quest to make him into her helpmate since I decided she needed his assistance. My fury grew with my determination to change Rob's behavior, even though no one else seemed bothered—which made me want to change their behavior too! Finally, exasperated, I left the scene and went to our own room for quiet reflection. When Laura came to get me for dinner, I laughed a little, saying, "I tried to guilt your husband into helping you, but that was a failed effort." And guess what she said? "Oh, he knows better than to interfere when I'm in the kitchen. He just gets in the way!"

The next morning, my husband and I were having early coffee with one of the guys, and he asked about this book, which I was then in the initial stages of writing. When I told him it was, among other things, about caretaking versus caregiving, explaining the difference between the terms to him, he said with a telltale grin, "So when you were trying to get Rob to help Laura last night, you were care*taking* Laura?" His astute words brought me up short, since he was right—I fit the definition to a T. I tried to control, I tried to manipulate, I tried to change what I could not, and I tried to fix what I determined needed fixing. I was embarrassed and so grateful that he trusted our forever friendship enough to call me on my actions. I apologized to everyone for allowing my need to control interfere with our time together, and was relieved when they treated it as no big deal. They probably shrugged off my actions as "It's just Cynthia being Cynthia," which lets me know I've got to keep practicing what I'm preaching.

When we use the Serenity Prayer as a reminder, we discover that the things we can change fall within our personal boundaries; the things we cannot change fall outside of them. When we practice boundary setting and maintenance, we usually discover that living with healthy boundaries is easier and better than living without them. Like everything in our journey from caretaking to caregiving, we can't expect to be the perfect boundary setters or keepers. Some of us may have gotten used to living with few, if any, boundaries, so this process can take lots of time and practice.

As my favorite Dove candy wrapper reminds, we are "fabulous and flawed," so try to go easy on yourself if you forget a boundary or step on someone else's from time to time. Boundary setting is a fluid and ongoing process. The best we can do is change what we can when we can change it and try to accept that those people we may want to change so badly are just as fabulous and flawed as we are.

As we will see in the next chapter, boundaries can help us get clearer on where we stand in the interconnected web of caregiving.

CHAPTER 4

The Circle of Care

*Caring is not a finite resource and, even more than that, it's like
a muscle. The more you exercise it, the stronger it gets.*
—JONATHAN SAFRAN FOER[1]

I like Foer's comparison of caring to a muscle that gets stronger
with exercise. Self-awareness, boundary keeping, and the other
elements of caregiving all take practice. When we exercise our
caring muscles, we're also practicing how to connect to others in
healthier and more fulfilling ways. This circle of connection can
expand and strengthen relationships and build a community that we
might want to call on when we need care ourselves.

Finding Our Place in the Circle of Care

In her wonderfully honest, poignant, and often funny book about
her own caregiving journey, author Susan Allen Toth talks about the
importance of having a caring circle in place.

> Many weeks ago, a friend sent me a supportive note, ending,
> "The net is larger than you imagine." I began pondering: where
> was my net? Because I had been so satisfied with my long,
> happy, and companionable marriage, I didn't weave a wide net
> beyond it. I do not belong to a particular church. I am not a

member of a book club, a garden club, a bridge club, or indeed any club at all. I don't like parties, and I haven't really entertained for years. I have a few close friends, but several now live in distant states or countries.

Last fall, Rachel, a visiting friend (one of those who had moved away), and I reconnected for lunch. We were talking about how hard it seemed at our age to make new close friends. "I ask myself sometimes," I told her, "now that James is unable to do it, who in the world would take me to a colonoscopy and then wait to take me home?" We laughed. Rachel said, "Well of course, I would, if I were here. But that's a good point. Who in Santa Barbara besides my husband would take me?" We agreed that we both needed to work harder to find friends who could pass the Colonoscopy Test.[2]

Finding our appropriate place in someone's circle (or net) of care and figuring out whom we would want in our own circle when we might need a helping hand is another way to establish and negotiate boundaries.

One way to do this is to use what psychologist Susan Silk calls the Ring Theory. Although the idea of using concentric circles to illustrate degrees of connection is not a new idea or unique to caregiving, I like how Silk explains hers. She came up with the Ring Theory when she was recovering from breast surgery and one of her colleagues said she wanted—she *needed*—to visit her. When Silk told her she wasn't up to having visitors, her colleague's amazing response was, "This isn't about you." In an op-ed piece coauthored with Barry Goldman for the *Los Angeles Times*,[3] she described how this theory could work in situations like this as well as in a number of other helping situations. This idea really hit home when I shared it with my caregivers' group. We discovered how easily it could be adapted for both care receivers *and* caregivers who might need some extra help and support themselves.

I've found it is a great way to figure out what boundaries and roles seem most appropriate when we have the desire to help out.

And it is another way to help us sort out what is care*taking* and what is care*giving*. Of course, caring circles—and our places in them— change as circumstances shift and change.

Here's how I create a circle of care. When I want to figure out my place as a caregiver, I put the name of the care receiver in the middle ring. Then I draw another circle around the center circle. The person or persons closest to the receiver go in that circle; the next closest go in the next circle, and so on, with more distant friends, relatives, or acquaintances in the larger, outer circles. Then I study the circles and people I've listed and try to assess in which concentric circle I honestly think I fit.

Circle of Care

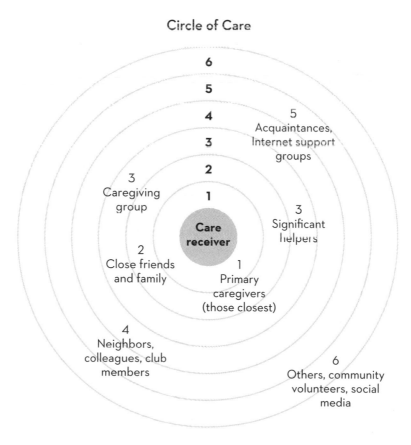

6

5

4   5
                          Acquaintances,
3   Internet support
                              groups
           3   2
       Caregiving
         group   1
                                        3
                                    Significant
                        Care   helpers
         2   **receiver**
     Close friends
      and family   1
                          Primary
                         caregivers
                       (those closest)

         4
     Neighbors,
  colleagues, club
      members   6
                              Others, community
                               volunteers, social
                                    media

If I had drawn a circle for my lifelong friends Ginny and Jack after Ginny was rushed to the hospital with a serious illness, I would put Ginny, as care receiver, in the middle of the circle, with Jack as primary caregiver in the first closest circle. They don't have children or close family, but they do have a big family of friends. I would put myself in the second circle with others I know who are just as close. Other significant (but not intimate) friends would be in the third, Ginny's coworkers and exercise group would go in the fourth, the online support group that helped Jack so much would go in the fifth. It seemed like everyone in and beyond their small town knew and loved Ginny, so they and all the hundreds of friends on her Caring-Bridge website would go in the sixth circle.

"Comfort In; Dump Out": The Art of Listening

Silk and Goldman say that when you are talking to a person in a ring smaller than yours (someone closer to the center), the goal is to help.

> Listening is often more helpful than talking. But if you're going to open your mouth, ask yourself if what you are about to say is likely to provide comfort and support. If it isn't, don't say it. Don't, for example, give advice. People who are suffering from trauma don't need advice. They need comfort and support. So say, "I'm sorry" or "This must really be hard for you" or "Can I bring you a pot roast?" Don't say, "You should hear what happened to me" or "Here's what I would do if I were you." And don't say, "This is really bringing me down."[4]

Like me, you may discover that you have intuitively used something like this Ring Theory in all sorts of situations without thinking much about it. For example, we'd probably not tell someone whose appearance has changed over time, "You look terrible," but we might express our concern to a mutual friend by saying, "I'm worried about Ian. He looks so thin and pale." Or we'd most likely censor ourselves from saying, "Well, if you hadn't smoked all those cigarettes," to an acquaintance who is recovering from heart surgery or who has just been diagnosed with lung cancer.

As Silk and Goldman put it, "Comfort in; dump out."[5] Imagine a friend who is going through a painful divorce. Since she and her children are the ones most affected, they would be in the innermost circle. Their feelings are probably all over the place, from grief to confusion to rage— but those are *their* feelings, and this is *their* loss. So it wouldn't be appropriate for those in the outer circles to "dump in" by saying in front of the children, "What a jerk. You are all better off without him," even though we might be very angry with him for walking out on this family we care about. Instead we listen. If we're close to the family, we might offer to do something fun with the kids like take them to a movie or a park so their mom can have some time for herself or if she feels the need to "dump out" to (or even with) another friend. If the kids want to talk, we listen to them, but we try to remember that we aren't their therapists, and they aren't our confidants. Or maybe we reassure them that they and their mom are loved and cared about by so many if they express worry or want to talk to us about the situation.

We all know how it feels *not* to be listened to—when we're in the middle of telling a story and a listener looks away, or gets up to get a beverage in the middle of our sentence, or interrupts us with their story or to make a point or argue. Here's what happened to Roger's dad.

ROGER'S STORY

My widowed elderly dad lives in a nearby care facility. He's still mentally sharp, but it's hard for him to get around, and he gets pretty lonely sometimes. His church has a great program called Befrienders, where trained volunteers visit people who would benefit from what they call a "listening presence," like Dad, or someone who is depressed or who has suffered a recent personal crisis or loss or life change. While they might play cards, or chat about something of mutual interest with the person they're visiting, or drive them to a doctor or the store, a Befriender is specifically taught not to advise, get entangled in family dramas, or talk about their own problems.

Well, my dad was teamed up with a Befriender, and it was going pretty good at first, and he seemed to enjoy the weekly visits. But after a while he started to complain how his Befriender volunteer was getting on his nerves. He'd tell me things like "She's so bossy. She tells me I shouldn't be taking the meds my doctor prescribed, and—even though she has no idea what she's talking about—she criticizes our family for not doing enough. Then she started asking about my finances." Dad got so upset after the last visit that I had to call the program director and ask for a different volunteer. The new one is terrific, and he loves visiting with him.

Roger's story underscores how important it is for persons being cared for to be listened to attentively, and John stressed this same thing in the previous chapter when he talked about how upset his teenage son got when he accused John of never listening to him. It takes practice and patience to become a "listening presence," but it is one of the most valuable skills a caregiver can have. If we learn to listen attentively, we often tune in to what people really need and want to talk about.

I like how Christina Baldwin explains the listening process. In her book *Storycatcher*,[6] she points out how the word *heart* contains the word *ear*. Deep listening is an art we can practice so when someone we are caring for is ready to talk, we'll be ready to listen in a nonjudgmental way with open heart, open mind, *and* open ears. This is often tougher than it sounds. It isn't easy to be an attentive listener in today's world filled with so much noise, so many distractions, and too much to do. Instead of emptying our minds so we can really *hear* what someone is saying, we are often so filled with the noise and busyness of our own lives that it's difficult to pay attention to what someone else is trying to say.

Attentive listening is a way to let someone know we think what they are saying is important enough to warrant our complete attention—which translates to we think *they* are important, which may just boost their self-esteem. I first learned the impact of listening many years ago when I had the opportunity to interview a woman who worked with the Passamaquoddy Indian Tribe in Pleasant Point, Maine. She told me the story of how eight Native Brothers, as they called themselves, opened up the gym three nights a week and made themselves available to the young people on the reservation who wanted to play sports or just talk. She said an average of forty-five kids showed up each night. Just three years before this program began, the tribe spent $13,300 on windows that some bored and angry children had vandalized. After the program was in place, they spent less than $100 on broken glass. These men not only modeled what it means to be a listening presence, they also modeled caregiving at its finest.

Luke still remembers the first time an adult took the time to really listen to him.

LUKE'S STORY

Coming home from Vietnam was more of an adjustment for me than going to war. I was so lost, I didn't even know I was lost. No one seemed to know what to say or how to act around me, and I couldn't relate to any of the friends whose lives now seemed so different than mine. My Uncle Nate, a World War II veteran, invited me to come and visit, and that visit changed my life. He didn't tell his war stories—he was just there—ready to hear mine if and when I was ready to tell them. And when I was finally ready to talk, he listened—without judgment, without interrupting, and without comparing our wars or our experiences. He seemed truly interested in and totally accepting of me. I felt cared for unconditionally. This experience shaped my life, and I even ended up following in his footsteps when it came to choosing a career.

Luke told me that when his uncle listened to him in such a deep and respectful way, he felt safe and was better able to sort out his thoughts and feelings. By attentively listening, Luke's Uncle Nate conveyed to him that he was interested in Luke as a person and he thought what Luke had to say was important.

Active listening is a skill that comes in handy anytime, but it is especially useful in caregiving situations. Here are some tips that I've adapted from a list of listening strategies I compiled for *Shock Waves*, a book I wrote about post-traumatic stress disorder (PTSD). You may find these helpful the next time you have an opportunity to practice being a listening presence:

- When someone seems to have something they need to talk about, try giving them your full attention by focusing on them and what they are saying. Turn off the television, the radio, and your computer, and turn toward the speaker so you can observe their body language. Be honest about your time. If you are in the middle of something that cannot be interrupted, apologize and schedule a time when you can give them your full attention and focus.

- Listening isn't only done with the ears; our body language, posture, and level of attentiveness all say something about our interest and concern. Show you are listening by asking for clarification when needed, by making eye contact, and by adding an occasional "uh-huh" or "I see," or by nodding your head.

- Show that you understand by occasionally restating (para-phrasing) what the other person has said by asking things like "Are you saying such and such?" or saying, "What I heard you say is . . ."

- Try to listen without judgment and resist the urge to inter-ject your opinion. Be aware of your personal triggers or filters—things that, because of your own experiences or history, might cause you to react with horror, anger, or fear.

If a powerful emotion arises that distracts you momentarily, it's okay to apologize by saying something like "I'm sorry. That part of your story struck an emotional chord for me that took me away for a second. Could you repeat your last sentence? I really want to hear what you have to say." Be honest if you need a break by saying something like "I'm really glad you're telling me about your experience, but this is hard for both of us, and I'm feeling a bit overwhelmed. Could we do this again tomorrow?"

- Resist saying, "I know how you feel."

- Make room for silence, and give the speaker time to gather their thoughts. It's fine to ask if they're done speaking before you respond.

- Resist the temptation to give advice.

- Validate the speaker's feelings by saying something like "That must have been difficult," or "That sounds really frightening."

- Finally, it's important to know when to back off. Pay attention to their body language as well as their words. If they seem agitated or emotionally overwhelmed, check in with them by asking how they're doing or if they want to take a break.[7]

When we participate in a caring circle, we join what a friend of mine calls the Sisterhood or Brotherhood of the Bloody Tongues, because sometimes it feels like we might bite our tongues right off when we want so much to jump in and offer our advice or opinion or tell our own stories. This doesn't mean we take a vow of silence. If we have information about a resource, a doctor, a medical treatment, a book, or something else that we think might be helpful and welcome, I think it's fine to check it out by saying something like "My brother had good luck with a new treatment regimen. I can send you information if you think it would be useful."

Once again, it comes down to trusting your best caregiving instincts and your ability to know whether you are being helpful or crossing a boundary. Well-meaning folks would often overwhelm Jack (of the Ginny/Jack story earlier) with tons of studies and advice, information about miracle cures, even conspiracy theories about why Ginny got terminally ill. To lessen the stress this was causing Jack, a few of us in the second circle became the research/response team. He would merely forward all the emails, calls, and letters to us, and we would take turns checking things out and responding on his behalf. It worked really well. We had his back, and the people who contacted him didn't feel ignored.

The caring circle idea can also help us respond appropriately in good news situations. I've seen it most often abused when a woman announces to her women friends that she is going to have a baby, and inevitably at least one of these friends will immediately start telling horror stories about her own pregnancy, labor, or delivery— which can scare the heck out of the new mom-to-be!

The overall point of this discussion is for caregivers to remember that when someone is in need of care, *they* get to occupy the center circle. What's going on is about them, not us—although there will be those care*takers* who want to jump into the spotlight and try to make it about themselves. Like most things that have to do with caregiving, these aren't rigid rules. Someone in a smaller circle than ours may *want* and ask for our opinion. They might want to know how what's going on with them is affecting us. They might ask if what is happening to them has ever happened to us. Or they may need a break from their own problems and look to us for relief or distraction by asking what's going on in our lives or wondering what they might do to help us. Much of the art of caregiving is about paying close attention to the cues a care receiver gives. Sometimes a person we're caring for may want to talk about the problem at hand; sometimes they may want to talk about something—anything—else. As we flex our caregiving muscles, we get more adept at reading these cues.

I'm a visual person, so the beauty for me of filling in a circle of care is that it also helps me not only see *where* I might help, but *whom* I might help. For instance, I may not really have a relationship with the person in the very center or even with their primary caregiver in the next closest circle, but I may have an intimate relationship with someone who occupies the next level of care.

This recently happened with dear friends whose brother-in-law has been diagnosed with terminal cancer. They are in one of the smaller circles of support for this family and, after a particularly long and emotionally draining day at the hospital, they called to ask if my husband and I could come over for a bite to eat and to play cards. "We really need to laugh a little," they said. When we got to their house, my husband wisely asked, "Do you want to talk about it?" They did—but only for a short while. So they talked and we listened. They cried, and we hugged them. Then we did play cards. And we did laugh, as we always do. I left, thinking how they had modeled both healthy caregiving *and* care receiving. They were clear about where they needed to be in the circle of care for their brother-in-law and his family, and where they needed us to be in our care for them.

From Listening to Doing

Although Silk's Ring Theory addresses what to say and what not to say to someone in need, I find that creating a circle of care can also be a very useful way to determine who might be best suited for caring tasks. While some caregivers might be shy about talking about or listening to feelings, they might relish the opportunity to show their care by mowing a lawn, fixing a meal, providing a ride, doing child care, or calling a plumber or car mechanic. Of course, there are those people who can jump from the emotional/listening circle of care to the practical/doing circle of care with ease. Some, like Deanna's friend, seem to intuitively know what is needed.

DEANNA'S STORY

Instead of asking what I needed or how she could help, a good friend would specifically ask if I'd like her to bring a dinner over.

*One night she told me she and her husband would be over to
clean the house while I took my husband to his chemo treatment
because she knew family would be arriving to stay with us. When
my mind was so preoccupied with his care, most of the time I had
no clue what we needed. Having her tell me specifically what she
wanted to do was a blessing!*

Deanna's friend knew where she wanted and needed to be in
Deanna's circle of care. She didn't intrude by expecting Deanna or
her husband to visit with her when they might be overwhelmed or
exhausted or busy with doctor appointments or other things. She
was content to play a supporting role by offering the sorts of practical things she thought would help the most.

Not surprisingly, some of those who offer care might place themselves in the inner circles of care, but the care receiver might not
consider them that close. It's not a perfect process, but it can be a
useful one if we approach it with honesty and humility, and if we
don't make too many assumptions about our relationship with the
person needing help.

Here's Ellen's experience when she was on the receiving end of
care.

ELLEN'S STORY

*The offer of help that nearly put me into orbit was a friend sug-
gesting that she "live in" for the duration of my recovery—which
took many months. I like her, but she would have driven my
partner and me a little nuts. I immediately improved—a lot! My
friends who really knew me were great. They said, "This is what
I'd like to do for you. How do you feel about it?"*

If you are confident of your closeness to the person in the center of the circle, or if they have specifically asked you to be one of
their primary caregivers, you might even want to have them fill out
a caring circle for themselves. This can help you and others in the

smaller circles get a clear picture of whom you could enlist to help when additional help is called for or offered. I think of those closest to the care receiver as the first "line of defense." With the circle in place, they'll also have a better idea of who the care receiver is most comfortable having do certain things. If necessary, these primary caregivers can screen unwanted calls or visitors. Favors that don't require a lot of personal interaction with the care receiver, like running errands, doing lawn care or certain household tasks, or coordinating meals, might go to those in the larger, outer circles. Evening visits, help with dressing or bathing, in-home meal preparation, and so on, would probably be handled more appropriately by those in the smaller, more intimate circles.

I urge you to play with this idea of creating a circle of care. (There is a circle of care template you can photocopy to fill out in appendix D.) Put the name of the person who is currently in need of care in the center circle (whether or not you have a personal relationship with this person), and then write in the names of those you think would occupy the next circle—those closest to the care receiver. Keep filling in each concentric circle until you get down to more distant friends, coworkers, or acquaintances. Don't worry if you don't know their names; just list things like "her relative in Ohio," or "his friend from the gym." Where have you placed your name? Would you most appropriately help the person in the center or someone in one of the concentric circles?

Now try this exercise by placing your own name in the center space and filling each concentric circle with those you would want as your primary caregiver(s) and those you would want to occupy each surrounding ring. Whom do you turn to first for comfort and support?

Do these two circles give you a clearer idea of whom you support and who supports you? To whom you would provide comfort and to whom you would "dump"? Does this visual give you a better idea of what kind of help you feel is most appropriate and most comfortable giving to someone in need?

Ultimately It's Kindness That Counts

As my psychologist friend explained, the whole issue of care—giving it and getting it—presses people to recognize that there are multiple layers of truth. The person giving care has their own sense of truth, and the person being cared for has their own truth. "Many truths can prevail, and a situation can be viewed through many lenses," she told me. "Our vigilance is imperfect, and sometimes caregivers anticipate needs, which can often be problematic. Anything that sounds like a recipe or a 'fix' might raise a red flag. Ultimately it's kindness from people that counts," she said.

Her wise and reassuring words bear repeating—especially when we unintentionally cross a boundary or make a wrong assumption. I've done this more than once, even when I wasn't being a needy care*taker,* and I'm guessing you may have too. When this happens, I try to remember what she said (especially when I'm caring for a somewhat "unlovable" person), "Ultimately it's kindness from people that counts." People can usually tell when another person's intentions are good ones and when they truly do have the care receiver's best interests at heart. Most people can tell the difference between kind intentions and selfish motives, so while it's good to be thoughtful about our place in the circle, I think it's important not to obsess about it or be so overly cautious that we don't extend a hand or open our hearts to someone in need.

As Ellen mentioned, if we aren't certain what our caregiving role should be, it's fine to check it out with the person you are caring for. You could say something like "I'm guessing this might be helpful, but I wanted to check it out first," or ask if you might bring dinner over on a specific night, as Deanna's friend did.

Figuring Out What Needs to Be Done

When it comes to giving care, two of the toughest questions people in need of help or support often get are "How can I help?" or "Is there anything I can do?" They might be in the midst of a crisis, depressed, physically and emotionally exhausted, or in pain. Or they might be someone who is very unused to accepting help. So often they don't have a clue what *they* should be doing, let alone what they'd like you to do. That's why Deanna's and Ellen's friends were so effective when they had specific ideas that they checked out with Deanna and Ellen.

It's difficult to anticipate what jobs might need to be done for someone, which is why I think it helps to imagine what we might need if *we* were the one who had fallen and broken a leg, who had just suffered a significant loss, who was feeling paralyzed by depression or loneliness, or who was expecting another baby. Maybe you've already been in a position where you needed to call on others for help so you have a good idea of what was useful and what could have worked better.

A list can help break down something big like "I NEED HELP!" into manageable parts by identifying what we might need, what we are able to do ourselves, and what we might need help doing. Making such a list before a crisis hits can save time, headaches, and even heartache because we have tasks, names of people, and numbers at our fingertips when they're needed.

I think this activity works well in conjunction with the caring circle because it can help the one in need of care better articulate what help is needed and who they might want to provide that help. It can also help caregivers get specific ideas of what kind of help they might want to offer and which things they are most comfortable doing. The beauty of a list is it can easily be altered or expanded at any time because we have a foundation in place on which to build.

We helped my sister do this when her husband of fifty years was diagnosed with a terminal illness. They lived in Florida, and the closest family member was an eight-hour drive away, so they both worried how she would be able to handle the numerous tasks involved with running a household on her own. We actually had fun compiling a manual of things—like which neighbor could help with lawn and pool care, whom to call for automobile care or advice, whom to call for a plumbing emergency or electrical outage or other emergencies, and where the circuit breakers were located.

My sister is a very competent person who could have figured all this out eventually, but she was already feeling overwhelmed with doctors' schedules, medication regimens, and tons of other caregiving duties, and tasks began to pile up as her husband's illness progressed. I think doing this while he was still able to participate gave him a sense of control and a feeling of reassurance. And I also think it afforded him an opportunity to think about something other than the uncertainty of what was coming. He was great. He directed us where he kept tools and equipment. He and my sister even made videos of how to change the pool filter and what to do in case of a power outage.

I encourage you to make your own list. For example, list whom would you most likely call

- to fix your washer, dryer, or some other appliance
- for an electrical problem
- for automobile maintenance, repair, or advice
- for lawn maintenance
- to help with a house project
- for a computer or Internet problem
- for telephone repair

This list doesn't only have to pertain to house or car maintenance. For example, you may want to list the person or people you would call

- in a health care emergency
- for financial or legal help
- to discuss a personal problem
- for emergency child care if you have young children
- for spiritual comfort or advice

- for a ride if your car broke down
- if you had an accident (e.g., insurance company, auto club, friend, or family member)
- for meals if you were injured or ill or overwhelmed with caregiving duties
- for a movie, a walk, a night out, or other fun activity
- to sit with a loved one if you were the primary caregiver and needed a break
- to pet-sit if you are suddenly called out of town
- for a long talk or a good laugh

What would you add to this list? Whom would you add? Were there any surprises? When you brainstorm your list, be sure to add names, emails, and phone numbers, and try to update the list and the contact information when things change. Include backup names and numbers whenever you think of them. Your list could even include things like the exact location of the circuit box, gas and water shut-offs, modem, tools, and other details that would make it easier for a person to help without having to ask fifty questions.

Once you've completed (or even thought about) your list of the people you might call for help when you might need it and filled in your own circle of care, think again about what kind of things— emotional support, task-oriented help, and so on—you see yourself giving to others.

I've always loved the story that Fred Rogers, star of the old public television children's show *Mr. Rogers' Neighborhood*, told many times.

> When I was a boy and I would see scary things in the news, my mother would say to me, "Look for the helpers. You will always find people who are helping." To this day, especially in times of "disaster," I remember my mother's words and I am always comforted by realizing that there are still so many helpers—so many caring people in this world.[8]

Creating a circle of care and listing those we might call upon in times of need or stress is a way to "look for the helpers." When we do these activities, we usually discover that "our nets are larger than we imagine," to paraphrase Susan Toth's friend in the beginning of this chapter. We find that we are surrounded by all sorts of helpers. We discover that, as caregivers, we are a part of a vast network of kindness and caring. This is community at its best. This is community in action.

Becoming sensitive to people's needs and more in tune to how we might best and most appropriately help those who may need our help is a way to cultivate compassion, which is the topic of the next chapter.

CHAPTER 5

Cultivating Compassion

If you come to me and say, "I'm depressed," and I touch
your pain, your depression, with fear, that's pity. . . .
But if I can touch your pain with love, that's compassion.
—STEPHEN LEVINE[1]

A mong other things, the last two chapters reinforced and built
upon the importance of establishing and maintaining appropriate boundaries in caring relationships. To paraphrase research
professor and best-selling author Brené Brown, better boundaries
make room for more compassion.[2] Compassion is at the heart of
caregiving and comes from a Latin word that means "to suffer with."
To me, *compassion* is a generous word that describes a quality that
allows people to tend to the needs of another while suspending their
need to control, fix, or manipulate.

Compassion bubbles in people like my Aunt Margaret. When her
daughter Chris was dying of a cancer that had invaded her lungs,
spine, and brain, Aunt Margaret packed her bags, drove the four
hours from St. Paul to Chris's home in Boone, Iowa, to practice
quiet, deep compassion. She bathed Chris, dressed her in soft fleece
sweatsuits, rubbed lotion on her smooth, bald head, soothed her,
and guarded her, leaving Chris's bedside only when she was sure
someone else was there to sleep on the pallet on the floor next to the
hospital bed Chris's husband set up in the living room.

When the pain got too great and the hospice nurses attached the morphine pump so Chris could press the button when she needed relief, it was Aunt Margaret who convinced Chris that it was okay to use it—even though Aunt Margaret knew the morphine would take her daughter even further from her. Day after day, my devoted aunt sat by Chris's bedside, listening calmly to morphine-laced dreams about missing babies and crowds of people speaking unintelligible languages, stroking Chris's hand and assuring her the dream baby was safe. Not only is my aunt a model of compassion, she is also the picture of empathy.

Empathy: The First Stop on the Road to Compassion

I've heard empathy commonly described as putting yourself in someone else's shoes, but I think it's more than that. Unless we're mind readers, we cannot know for certain what another person is feeling or thinking—even if we have experienced something similar to what they are going through. Our car accident is not their car accident; our illness is not their illness; our loss is not their loss—even though we might be grieving the same person or pet or thing. When something significant happens in our lives, we respond in our own unique way. Our own history, our own personality, our own understanding and knowledge, our own thoughts, and our own feelings shape the way we internalize and react to a situation or event.

The word *empathy* comes from a Greek work that means "in feeling" or "feeling into."

Unlike Commander Troi, the half-human, half-alien empath in the old science fiction television series *Star Trek: The Next Generation*, we normal human beings cannot literally feel *exactly* what another person is feeling. She had the ability to physically and psychically take on another's pain or anguish. To me, being "in feeling" means feeling *with* someone.

I don't mean to say that we can't be affected by what someone else is going through. When my husband first opened up to me about his experiences as a Marine in Vietnam, I was deeply affected by his stories. I could not *be* him, but I could be with him. Here's how I described this in previous writings:

> I listened to his stories deep into that night and began to ache from the weight of that terrible war. Of course, I couldn't know what it was like to actually be there, but his descriptions of burning villages made my eyes sting. I imagined the villagers hugging themselves tight in fear and grief, as I drew a blanket tightly around me. I still remember the name of the little cat—Titi Lau—that was eaten by the rats. As he talked, I felt like I walked in jungle heat with him. Through his eyes, I saw two little boys get ripped apart by machine guns after they set off a homemade bomb that killed Michael's fellow Marines.
>
> Michael put the photographs back into their envelope, stuffing them and the memories away in his sea bag, and we didn't talk about these things until years later. But the stories and images stayed with me and even invaded my dreams on occasion. I was glad Michael trusted me enough to tell me his war stories, but in gaining his confidence I also lost something that night. The world seemed more fragile, less certain; a darker place where little boys and 19-year-olds could be made to kill and be killed. I grew more protective of our daughter, and more fearful for myself and those I loved.[3]

When Michael was diagnosed with PTSD many years later, I learned the hard way about healthy balance and boundaries and the difference between "care*taking* empathy" and "care*giving* empathy." I was definitely on the care*taking*/enmeshed side of the continuum discussed in previous chapters when he had an emotional crash and began intensive therapy. I wanted so desperately to support this man I loved, becoming so tangled up in what he was going through that I also ended up in therapy for depression. I made the initial appointment thinking I would get help with how I might best support Michael, but when my intuitive therapist asked, "But who is helping you with *your* war?" I broke down sobbing, and, with her guidance, came to realize that I could not genuinely care for and support my husband if I was not taking good care of myself. I learned I could hear his story without *becoming* his story. That, to me, is caregiving and healthy empathy. It involves self-care (which we'll go into more deeply in upcoming chapters) and good balance and boundaries.

When we practice "boundaried empathy" with someone, we can open ourselves to compassion. We are, as Stephen Levine describes it in the above epigraph, able to touch their pain with love. We can listen attentively and pay attention to their body language to get a sense of how deeply a trauma or event is affecting them. We can hold them, cry or laugh with them, comfort them, and support them. We can feel *with* them.

Here's how Suzanne described her personal journey in empathy and caregiving.

SUZANNE'S STORY

One of my new lines is "everyone has their shit." Everyone's stuff is different, and this is the difficult stuff we're dealing with right now. I try to remember that everyone everywhere is struggling with some difficulty a lot of the time, from worrying about grown children's issues, a grandchild with strep throat, or an ailing parent. Everyone cares deeply about something that isn't going well in their lives. Everyone is hurting, struggling, tired in some sense, and we need to be the kindest person we can be at every opportunity. One bright person in a grocery line can brighten my day. I want to be that for someone else. So my mantra is, "Let me bring light to someone else. Let me be less critical and judging and more accepting. Let me be a better version of me. Let this experience enable me to hold someone else up through their journey in a better way. Let me be a better listener and offer fewer solutions. Let me help someone else suffer less some of the time. Let me be a better person." I guess that is what I want from this experience in caregiving.

In an article titled "What Is Empathy?"[4] experts at the University of California, Berkeley's Greater Good Science Center explain the difference between "affective empathy" (sometimes called "emotional empathy") and "cognitive empathy." According to them, affective empathy relates to the feelings we have in reaction to other people's emotions. They write that "this can include mirroring what that person is feeling, or just feeling stressed when we detect another's fear or anxiety." They state that cognitive empathy, which is sometimes called "perspective taking," is about "our ability to identify and understand people's emotions."

Reading facial expressions is one way to test and practice empathy, and the Greater Good Science Center developed a free and fun online multiple choice quiz at www.greatergood.berkeley.edu /ei quiz/ that shows twenty photos of people registering various emotions like happiness, anger, sadness, or fear.[5] The object is to guess which emotion you think is being conveyed. When you make your choice and click "Get the Answer," the quiz makers explain which facial muscles convey which emotion and describe the subtle differences between expressions. I encourage you to copy and paste the above address or do a search for "Greater Good Body Language Quiz" to see how well you read other people. Although I only scored "slightly better than average," I find it reassuring that they say research shows we can improve with practice.

The Evolution of Empathy

Many researchers and experts in the fields of neuroscience and animal behavior assert that humans and many other mammals are "wired" for empathy, that it comes from a part of the brain that has evolved throughout the centuries. In humans, exceptions can exist for people who have autism or a personality disorder such as schizophrenia, psychopathy, or borderline personality disorder. We certainly don't have to look far to find examples that support this "brain claim." Think of the television specials about chimpanzees or other primates that show these animals exhibiting concern for each other or the humans with whom they interact. Or think of the stories of dolphins rescuing people whom they sense are in danger and the therapy dogs in hospitals that soothe and delight both young and old patients. Or think about the pets you have known. Sandy's experience is a moving example of this.

SANDY'S STORY

We used to have a wonder dog named Maxine and a unique cat named Antoinette who grew up together. One day Max got hit by a car and had to spend a month with a leg cast on. From the moment Max got home from the vet's office, Toni the cat would not leave her side. She slept in the dog bed with her buddy. She licked Max's leg and face. It seemed like she sensed that Max was hurting, and she wanted to comfort her. A few years later, our daughter was born. That dog would never leave that baby's side. She would guard the stairway when our daughter began crawling, she would stay especially close to her when she cried, and she would lie beside her crib at naptime. Those two were inseparable until the day Maxine died when our daughter was a teenager.

Apparently, some birds also exhibit empathy-like behavior. Just recently I heard about Serenity Park, a sanctuary in Los Angeles that cares for abandoned or rescued parrots. Its founder, Lorin Lindner, is a clinical psychologist who also started a program for homeless veterans called New Directions. On a particularly frustrating day in group therapy when she felt she was getting nowhere with the vets she was counseling, she decided to take them with her to the parrot sanctuary to help build more aviaries for the increasing number of parrots who needed care. As she recounted in a *New York Times* article,[6] "All of a sudden these same tight-lipped guys are cuddling up to the parrots and talking away with them." The traumatized birds took comfort from the traumatized vets, and the vets were comforted by the birds. It was an unspoken but remarkable example of an "inter-species" exchange of mutual comfort that is now a regular part of Lindner's PTSD therapy. Other people have told me of similar breakthroughs they've had in therapy programs that team people with physical and mental conditions with horses.

Of course, other experts point out that what looks like empathy in nonhumans is usually based on observation and anecdotes and more likely stems from an ingrained instinct to protect a member of the group because the group was made stronger and had better chances of survival when *all* of the members lived to protect and contribute. They caution that our tendency and desire to assign human traits and emotions to nonhumans—which is called *anthropomorphism*—can be misleading or even dangerous because we expect cuddly animals to act like humans and get disappointed when they still act like animals. Perhaps to Maxine, the attentive dog in the above story, Sandy's daughter was a member of her pack that she instinctively cared for. Just because Maxine protected one baby doesn't mean she would care for all babies.

I won't go into the neuroscientific studies about the areas of the brain that are linked to compassion and empathy in humans, but I do find them fascinating. And they make such sense to me. All I have to do is watch how babies respond to those who laugh or coo or comfort them to believe that we are born with brains that contain the seeds of empathy within them. This gets reinforced when I watch how toddlers seem to sense when one of their little friends is upset or lonely or in need of a hug. For that matter, all I have to do is tune in to my own reactions when I see or read something that tugs my heartstrings to the point of tears to believe that we have the *capacity* for empathy—even if that something is a commercial I know is designed to manipulate my emotions.

But I also believe that even if we do have the capacity to empathize, it also takes self-awareness and practice to fine-tune our empathetic natures—especially when it comes to caregiving. In fact, doing favors, volunteering, caring for and about others, and just plain being kind are all ways to practice empathy and strengthen our ability to empathize. As the familiar saying goes, "If we don't use it, we lose it." Here's how Bob explained his approach to caring for those who need help.

BOB'S STORY

I am a son, a brother, a neighbor, a colleague, and a member of a church community. All my acquaintances (whether I love them or merely like them) are mortal and, as such, from time to time need help. I help them because I am part of them. They are a part of me. I think of caregiving and care receiving as inevitable components of Life.

Sometimes caregiving means just being with someone. It's not having a conversation per se; it's about the gradual knowing that comes from paying attention to the other person—tuning into their sometimes unspoken values, fears, hopes, etc. I read a book by Jean Stairs called Listening for the Soul *when I was first recruited to join our church's pastoral care team, and I've re-read it twice since then. The author calls for developing a sense of deeper listening for the feeling or message that is just under the surface of the conversation; how this is an observation of body language.*

Recent studies also show how our own emotions can affect our capacity to empathize with another person. For example, when we are feeling great and happy, it is often more difficult to empathize with someone who is in distress or pain. On the other hand, if we have just suffered something distressful ourselves, we run the risk of thinking another person's difficulty might not be as bad as it actually is. This is a good reason for caregivers to check in with themselves to make sure they are able to be truly present with someone who is in need of a shoulder or a listening ear. This checking-in process is often called "emptying your cup."

The idea of emptying your cup is often linked to the Buddhist story about the Zen master and the scholar who came to the great teacher full of enthusiasm and ideas, eager to impress him with all that he had learned about Zen already—all the places he had studied and the knowledge he had gained along the way. As he rambled, the master poured tea into the student's cup. As he talked and talked, the master poured and poured, until the student shouted in alarm, "Stop! The cup is already full!" To which the master replied, "You are like this cup. You come to learn, but make no room for anything else because your cup is already too full. Before you can hear, before you can learn, you must empty your cup."

I consider emptying our cups an important element of healthy caregiving. Our intentions can be so honorable and our heart in the right place. But I don't believe we can be truly *with* someone if we come with a "cup" filled with our own concerns, opinions, attitudes, or distractions that get in the way of our ability to listen attentively. I know how I feel if I am disturbed and a well-meaning friend invites me to share what's going on, only to interrupt me with her own concerns or to argue, lecture, or respond with a message that conveys "just get over it." It would be interesting (and probably shocking) to do a survey on how many deep conversations have been interrupted by texts and cell phones!

I think that emptying our cups is a practice in empathy that can help us be more present with someone we are caring for so we can do the type of deep listening Bob describes above. However, empathy doesn't require person-to-person contact. Empathy can also be communicated in phone conversations or in sending a note or an email—but so can distraction and dismissiveness. Here's how Thomas recalled his experience.

THOMAS'S STORY

Most people I know, including myself, belittle their painful experiences because we all know someone who has it worse. When I had a breakdown, part of my therapy was to acknowledge and honor my feelings. My therapist helped me expose my anger, embarrassment, guilt, and confusion so that I could no longer deny my suffering, so that I could swim in it instead of being drowned by it. I had become pretty isolated and finally worked up the courage to reach out to others. I started by answering an email I had gotten months before from a lifelong friend. Although our lives had taken different turns, Jane and I had kept in touch over the years, and she had sent me a warm note asking how I was doing. I told her I was pretty messed up, that I had been hospitalized for severe depression, but that I was working hard in therapy and feeling a little more human every day.

She wrote back right away: "I am so sad for you and all you're going through, but at least you're alive. Be grateful, move on, and try to be happy. I continue praying for you that your journey will bring you to the Truth whose name is Jesus. All you really need to do is accept Christ as your Lord, and all will be healed."

Her email sent me reeling. I felt dismissed and insulted and angry. I was working so hard in therapy, and here she was telling me to take a "pill" and get over it—only in this case the pill was religion. Her religion. Maybe she thought that saving my soul was a way to show she cared, but it sure didn't feel that way.

At the church I attend in St. Paul, the ministers invite those in attendance into a space of unity and mutual support by reminding them, "Your gifts and your wounds are welcome here." That to me is the message of empathy. It is a nonjudgmental message that communicates our willingness to stand by, to be with another in their moments of pain and in their moments of celebration. As David discovered, this isn't always easy.

DAVID'S STORY

I befriend a lot of angry combat vets—young and old, men and women. As a war vet myself, I can relate to their feelings; I'm still bitter about the wounds—psychic and physical—that so many of us carry. One of my friends suffers from chronic pain from his war injuries. He can no longer work, which sucks, because he was self-employed. He lost his house as a result, so now he's homeless, and it's a full-time job going to medical appointments and fighting the powers that be for more benefits. I've spent countless hours with him, but it's hard to be in the presence of a person who is so pissed off at the world—even though I certainly understand his anger. But in my heart, I know I'm making his life a little less miserable just by simply listening and sharing a little of his burden.

Pause for a moment and think of your own experiences in empathy. Have there been times when you have taken in someone's pain or feelings to the point that it was affecting your own feelings or behavior? Have there been times when you've been unable to be fully present with someone because something was on your mind to the point of distraction? Can you think of a time when you have been able to listen attentively and be genuinely *with* someone in need? Is there a time when you were shown true empathy? How did that feel?

We can practice empathy by emptying our own cup, slowing down, and paying close attention to what someone is saying and how they are saying it. Being mindful in this way can help lessen the distractions that might interfere with our ability to fully be with another person. We can talk less and listen more, trying our best to suspend judgment, not rushing to conclusions or diminishing someone's experience by treating it too lightly. We can try our best not to offer pat advice or empty consolations like "*at least* you're alive," as Jane did in Thomas's story.

The Importance of Empathy in Caregiving

The experts at the Greater Good Science Center point out how empathy can foster more successful relationships because it helps us better understand the views, needs, and intentions of others. They recap current research that underscores the far-reaching effects that practicing empathy can have.[7] For example, the studies they reviewed show the following:

- People who exhibit a high degree of empathy are more likely to help others, even when doing so is not in their own self-interest.

- Empathy can help reduce prejudice and racism. It can also help fight inequality because it encourages our desires to help those in need who are not in our social group. (On the other hand, studies also show that inequality can reduce empathy among those who attain a higher economic status.)

- Empathy can be good for a marriage (I take this to mean any committed relationship) because it deepens intimacy and aids in conflict resolution.

- Empathy can reduce bullying among children because it promotes kindness and decreases aggression.

- Empathy can make for a better work environment. For instance, empathetic managers were shown to have happier employees who were sick less often.

- Empathetic doctors were shown to be more content and to have healthier and more satisfied patients.

In sum, healthy empathy—which I described above as "boundaried" because it allows us to offer genuine comfort and understanding to others without getting overwhelmed or overtaken by the other person's feelings or experience—has benefits that extend far beyond caregiving. But caregivers who regularly exercise their "empathy muscles" will particularly benefit as they discover how being *in feeling* with another person allows them to act with more compassion, patience, understanding, and kindness. This is what Paul discovered.

PAUL'S STORY

When I've been able to suppress my tendency to offer suggestions and advice, I think I can be a good listener. I'm not very good at making meals or doing house maintenance when it comes to caregiving, but I believe others can be open with me. My brother had a pretty tricky, life-threatening operation recently, and I think that being at the hospital day after day, watching and developing an understanding of what he was experiencing, allowed me to be more empathetic. Some people who visited seemed really uncomfortable or so overwhelmed by their own emotions they looked like they wanted to bolt. I'm guessing they might have been thinking, "If this can happen to someone in such good shape, it can happen to anyone; it could happen to me." Some people cried and voiced their sadness and worry about how this must be affecting his wife and kids and young grandkids. He told me it sometimes felt like they expected him to comfort them, so he often pretended he was dozing off just so they'd leave. He was worried enough already about what would happen if he didn't make it. Others tried to lighten the seriousness by telling jokes (which he actually seemed to enjoy). Anyway, I learned a lot from observing these interactions. I felt good that he opened up with me, and I did my best to just be present with him.

Perhaps the people who upset Paul's brother might have benefited by learning about the circle of care described in the previous chapter (see pages 73–90) and the "comfort in/dump out" rule associated with it. As care receiver, Paul's brother was in the center of the circle; the visitors, however, occupied one of the outer rings, so it was inappropriate to "dump in" to him. Instead of expressing their worry or sorrow directly to Paul's brother, they could have discussed their concerns with someone less intimately involved in the crisis of the moment—someone in one of the larger circles.

It is so easy—and normal—to be engulfed by the deep emotions that rush to the surface when we are with someone in pain. When this happens to me, thoughts of dread or despair—thoughts like "What if?," "What will the others do?," "What will I do?"—race through my mind and escape to my tongue if I don't catch them in time. To prevent this, I find it helps to bite my tongue and silently repeat to myself, "When in doubt, dump out; when in doubt, dump out," until I have a quiet moment in which to reflect and sort out my feelings and figure out in whom I can confide.

A Closer Look at Compassion

Mother Teresa, the famous Catholic nun who achieved sainthood and a Nobel Peace Prize for the charitable work she did among the poor and suffering in India, is said to have called compassion "love in action." I like this definition, especially because it gives me a way to distinguish empathy from compassion. Although the two emotions are definitely interrelated, I think of empathy as more static—more of a "love in *being*" versus a "love in *action*." That's why I called empathy the first stop on the road to compassion. While empathy is feeling and being *with*, I view compassion as the next step—the reaching out and doing. As Brené Brown says, "Empathy is the skill set to bring compassion alive."[8]

As I understand it, compassion encompasses empathy but can include *doing* as well as *being*. In other words, we can be empathetic and compassionate at the same time. Here's my example of what this means in real life. I met Rhonda when I first joined a care team at our church. This was a group of volunteers who helped church members when they needed a favor, some care, or company—new parents who often felt overwhelmed in those first weeks after a baby arrives; people in hospitals or nursing homes; people recovering from an illness, operation, or injury; people coping with loss or change. Rhonda was one of the vibrant team leaders and an expert when it came to compassionate caregiving. However, like so many proficient caregivers, she struggled with receiving care and comfort herself when she, at just thirty-six, was diagnosed with an inoperable, very aggressive brain tumor she dubbed "Stella" because it was shaped like a star.

Rhonda and her husband were both self-employed musicians and music teachers with minimal insurance, so it was especially tough for them when she had to quit working. Her devoted husband tried his best to manage everything while working long and irregular hours, but all the minutiae of scheduling appointments and making calls robbed him of precious time with her. Fortunately, her sister was able to get a leave from her own job when Rhonda needed round-the-clock care, and many of us also pitched in to help out— which was okay with Rhonda since she saw this as a way to help her husband and sister.

As devastating as the whole situation was, it was always a joy to be with Rhonda. As her cancer progressed, she had greater difficulty staying on track, but would frequently surprise me with some piece of wisdom, like the day she told me to "follow your fear," or the time she whispered, "Loving you is like loving the rain." "Rhonda has one foot in this world and one foot in the next right now," our minister Janne explained. She urged me "to let the mystery be," to be present with open heart and mind, even when things didn't always make sense. "All we can do is listen and love and play it as it comes," she said. Although I didn't realize it at the time, she was describing important elements of both empathy (listening with open heart and mind) and compassion (playing it as it comes).

Not long after this conversation, Janne and I went together to deliver a "Caring Hands Quilt" our quilters had made for Rhonda out of colorful squares that contained the patterns of hands that some of our adults and children traced onto them. When we arrived with the quilt and a coffee cake, Rhonda's sister answered the door in tears, blurting, "Rhonda rolled out of bed during her sponge bath, and I can't lift her by myself so she's sitting on the floor until the paramedics get here."

That's when I witnessed what Janne meant by "playing it as it comes." She tenderly wrapped the quilt around Rhonda's bare shoulders and, not missing a beat, asked, "Is the coffee on? We can have a tea-party picnic until they get here!" Rhonda loved this idea, so we got the cups, the coffee, and the coffee cake and gathered around her on the bedroom floor for our spontaneous party. I'm sure the paramedics who arrived to help get her back into bed were surprised to see four women on the floor chatting merrily and munching strudel.

I marveled at Janne's unruffled presence and the way she protected Rhonda from embarrassment and lessened everyone's anxiety. This was compassionate caregiving. This was love in action.

Empathy-Based Compassion

If empathy is *feeling with,* and compassion is *responding to,* I would say that Janne modeled what I see as the heart of caregiving: empathetic compassion. She didn't treat Rhonda as a victim, an incapacitated child, or "the other." She treated her respectfully and didn't make a big deal out of what could easily have been a humiliating experience for our dear friend. She took it in stride, which encouraged all of us to do the same—including the paramedics who handled everything as smoothly as if it were no big deal (which it probably wasn't for them). Although this happened over ten years ago, the caregiving lessons I learned that day have stayed with me. Since then, others, like Jen, have shared similar stories.

JEN'S STORY

One of my coworkers was injured in a cliff-diving accident he had as a boy. As a result, he is quadriplegic and in a wheelchair. He has a little use of his hands, and although he manages most things really well—including the competitive archery he does with a special bow—some fine motor tasks are difficult for him. But I've never heard him ask for help, and I've always been shy about offering to do things because he strikes me as such a proud guy. Some of us, including Ray, occasionally go out for lunch together, and I've come to notice how another friend always manages to sit by him. Steve never makes a big deal out of it, but, without even a break in conversation, he'll casually help Ray when a piece of food needs cutting or bread needs buttering. It's so natural and discreet; I just recently realized that's why he sits there. It struck me as such a kind and respectful way to care for someone. Watching this has helped me be more relaxed—more "natural"—around Steve and others who have physical or mental challenges. It served as such an important reminder to focus on the person—not his or her disability.

What about Sympathy?

In the introduction to this book, I talked about how easy it is to get hung up on words, but as I stressed, I view words as "fingers" that can direct us toward understanding, and that understanding can lead to the sense of connection that occurs when we know we're speaking the same language. The differences in the terms discussed in this chapter are subtle, but I think it's important to explore those differences because such an exploration can help peel the layers of the caregiving experience. I find that naming my feelings increases my self-awareness—especially when it comes to caregiving. It is a way for me to check in with myself. To make sure I am maintaining a healthy balance, I might ask myself, "Am I expressing genuine empathy or crossing a boundary?" "Am I being compassionate or am I caretaking by trying to fix or solve the problem?"

Depending on the situation and my relationship with the person, there are times when a less involved expression of sympathy feels like the more appropriate response in a caring situation. While *sympathy* is often used interchangeably with *empathy* or *compassion*, I consider it to be a little less intimate. Although some who have written on the subject talk a bit unfavorably about it, I do not consider sympathy as a negative response to someone's misfortune or pain.

Unlike pity, which usually describes a "one up/one down" response (e.g., "I feel so bad for the starving children in Ethiopia"), to me an expression of sympathy is an acknowledgment that you realize that someone is going through a difficult time. For example, we might say to a coworker or acquaintance, "I am so sorry about the loss of your father." Or we might send a card or brief note of sympathy or support to someone when we want them to know they are in our thoughts or prayers but when we don't share the sort of relationship where we would get emotionally involved on a more intimate level.

Of course, there are perfectly appropriate *acts* of sympathy as well as *expressions* of sympathy. Joan's story illustrates what I mean.

JOAN'S STORY

> *I'm pretty introverted when it comes to reaching out to people I don't know very well. But I enjoy doing things like sending cards, making a donation, or preparing an occasional meal when I learn that someone I know casually is ill or going through a tough time. For instance, my women's club, which has over seventy-five members, often puts the word out in an email or in their newsletter that a member could use some sort of support. Sometimes they coordinate fund-raisers or meal drop-offs or ask us to send notes of cheer or sympathy when one someone has experienced a significant life event. This involvement—even though it is sort of "arm's-length"— makes me feel a part of a supportive community, and I know from personal experience when I was in the hospital how getting lots of cards from group members (many of whom I didn't know personally) can cheer someone up and make them feel supported.*

I think Joan's story points out how even "casual caregiving" can brighten someone's day and strengthen the bond of community. And I like her reminder that while we may choose not to get personally involved in someone's care or if doing so might feel awkward or inappropriate because we don't know them that well, we can still send a note or card.

When someone dies, knowing what to say in a sympathy note or card can often be tricky. Although there are, no doubt, other Internet sites that offer suggestions, I found some helpful hints at the Hallmark greeting card company site at ideas.hallmark.com /sympathy-ideas/what-to-write-in-a-sympathy-card/ that you might want to check out if you, like many of us, sometimes struggle with what to say or write to someone who has suffered a loss.[9] Of course what and how much you say depends on your relationship with the individual or family. I won't replicate the entire list, but some of their suggestions are

- We are sorry for your loss.
- With deepest sympathy.
- It was truly a pleasure working with your father for seventeen years. He will be deeply missed.
- Thinking of all of you as you celebrate your grandmother's remarkable life.
- Our family is keeping your family in our thoughts and prayers.

They suggest that if you knew the deceased but not the family members, it might be helpful to include a brief note to mention your connection, as the coworker did in the example above. Survivors also may enjoy hearing a fond (brief) memory or how you admired the person who died. A few of Hallmark's examples are

- What a good and generous man your father was. I thought his funeral service was a wonderful tribute to him and all he has done for our community. He will be missed.
- Your daughter touched so many lives for the good. I'm grateful I had the chance to know her both as a colleague and a friend.
- I have the best memories of Aunt Edie—like the times when she would take us to Becker's for ice cream. I'm going to miss her fun-loving spirit.

Thank goodness the Hallmark folks also include examples of what *not* to write in a sympathy card. As they say, some thoughts or phrases might minimize the recipient's unique feelings of grief and run the risk of hurting someone's feelings or adding to their pain. The examples and rationale they include are

- I know how you feel. (We all experience and process grief differently.)

- She was so young. (No need for a potentially painful reminder.)

- What a terrible loss. (Avoid dwelling on the pain or difficulty of the loss.)

- You should . . . (Instead of advice, offer comfort and support.)

- You will . . . (Steer clear of predictions about how their grief journey will go.)

- This happened for a reason. (Even with the best intentions behind it, this thought risks assigning blame for the death.)

Ultimately, It's about Kindness

To sum up the above discussion about words and their meanings, here's how I personally define the following concepts in my own little "caregiving dictionary":

- Sympathy is the *acknowledgment* of someone's pain, difficulty, and loss. I think of an expression or act of sympathy as a way to provide comfort and support without getting intimately or emotionally involved as a caregiver.

- Empathy means to *feel with* someone. Empathy is "love in *being*"—a nonjudgmental and accepting caregiving response that allows us to view things from another person's perspective. When we practice empathy, we pay attention to a person's body language, listen deeply and attentively, and are fully present with them without interjecting our opinions or advice.

- Care*taking* empathy is an enmeshed, "unboundaried" response in which we get so overly involved in someone's story or plight that we "take on" their emotions; we risk getting depressed or so weighed down by our feelings that it can compromise our ability to be a compassionate care*giver*.

- Compassion is, in the words of Mother Teresa, "love in *action*." Compassion is a generous quality in which caregivers tend to a person's needs, without attempting to fix or control them or the situation.

- Empathetic compassion is the marriage of empathy and compassion, a caregiving response that involves *being* as well as *doing*. When we practice empathetic compassion, we remain fully present and feel with a person while we compassionately respond to their needs.

As I've already stressed, these terms as I've defined them can overlap and meld. Sometimes we choose to respond with sympathy, sometimes we elect to just be with someone in need, and sometimes we are moved to action. Other times, we might find ourselves on a caretaking continuum that moves from acknowledgment of, to feeling with, to doing for. There is no one-size-fits all formula or perfect response. As long as we respond with loving-kindness and with an open heart and mind, I have every confidence we will grow stronger in our ability to be more compassionate caregivers.

As I wrote about empathy, compassion, and sympathy, a line from a very old poem I wrote for a friend kept going through my mind: "Why do you weep? Compassion for others, or sacrificed self?" Too often, we care for others and forget to care for ourselves.

I fervently believe that a huge part of compassionate caregiving is remembering to give ourselves the same quality of sympathy, empathy, and compassion that we are striving to give others. This is why the next chapter is devoted to the importance of self-care.

Joys, Challenges, and the Importance of Caring for Ourselves as We Care for Others

*It's like if you were walking outside in a thunderstorm, umbrella-less,
and you walked into a café filled with plush armchairs, wicker baskets
full of flowers, and needlepoints on the walls that say things like
"Be kind to yourself" and "You are enough." It's jarring, the change
in scenery, but nice. It also makes you realize that you're soaked—
you'd almost gotten used to it, out in the storm.*

—JULIE BECK[1]

The paradox of choosing to practice what I described as "empathetic compassion" in the preceding chapter is that such an act has the potential to fill you up both emotionally and physically or suck you dry. I know that if I'm doing my care*giver* best—respecting both my own and another's boundaries, acting with intention and self-awareness, recognizing my own limits, and trying to maintain a healthy balance—I generally emerge from a caring experience energized and satisfied. I feel good about the interaction and usually feel closer to the person I'm helping.

However, if I slip into my all-too-familiar care*taker* ways, acting or committing to help someone without thinking it through—for example, saying yes when I already had too much on my plate or my motives were debatable—I often emerge feeling somewhat anxious, often regretting that I had not made better choices. In those instances, I also find it's easy to let some resentment creep in.

Sometimes, as Lance found out, doing favors can hold a mixture of frustration and satisfaction all at the same time.

LANCE'S STORY

I love computers and I love people, which means that I'm often the go-to guy when it comes to questions about how a certain program works or why something won't work the way it's supposed to work. When Mom was alive, I used to get so many calls—"How do I do that again? How come I can't get online?" And for every call I got from her, I'd get just as many from her senior friends. I usually got a kick out of it. I mean, here they were, this group of lively folks who grew up before television, learning to communicate in an entirely new way with tools they never dreamed of. I work out of my home, though, and to be honest, I would just cringe when one of those calls came in and I was in the middle of a work project. I'd get so impatient having to go over things once again or irritated by some of their silly questions. Of course, I didn't have the heart not to answer the phone, which probably says more about me than them. Now since Mom's gone, I sort of miss those calls. I'd give anything to hear her voice again.

As mentioned in the previous chapter, most humans have the capacity and instinct for empathy and compassion. However, that doesn't mean we all choose to act on those instincts. Let's face it: Putting ourselves out there can be risky business. As Lance related, sometimes agreeing to do a favor can feel like an imposition. It takes time, energy, and a good dose of self-confidence to care for others, so why do it?

This chapter hopes to answer that question by taking an honest look at the benefits and challenges of caregiving. It will also discuss how practicing good self-care can help prepare us for many of the caregiving challenges that may come our way so we can get more joy and fulfillment out of a caregiving experience. As has been the case so far, this discussion pertains to all kinds of caregiving situations. We'll take a deeper look at the unique aspects of caring for a loved one with a serious injury, illness, or condition in upcoming pages.

Why Should We Care?

It's true that without safeguards or appropriate assistance in place, caring for others can take a serious toll. Yet recent studies show that—generally speaking—helping others has numerous benefits. For instance, the 2013 study I mentioned in the introduction that Michael Poulin and other researchers conducted over a five-year period showed that helping others can protect our health by lessening the negative effects of stress and lengthening our lives.[2]

But the positives don't stop there. The 2007 U.S. Government report produced by the Corporation for National and Community Service[3] reviewed decades of research that illustrated the health, social, and political benefits of volunteerism. As was the case with the Poulin study, the government report underscored that even when controlling for factors such as age, health, and gender, individuals tend to live longer when they help others. Longevity isn't the only benefit that comes from helping others. The report concludes by stating:

> While these studies may differ in terms of their specific findings, they consistently demonstrate that there is a significant relationship between volunteering and good health; when individuals volunteer, they not only help their community but also experience better health in later years, whether in terms of greater longevity, higher functional ability, or lower rates of depression. In addition, we present first-time evidence that when a state has high volunteer rates, they are more likely to have greater longevity and less incidence of heart disease.[4]

In other words, when you help, helping helps you and makes for a healthier community. The studies show there is less depression, more sense of purpose, greater life satisfaction and happiness, higher self-esteem, and better physical health among those who offer service to others. These positive effects are also prevalent among those with chronic or serious illnesses. For instance, studies found that persons suffering from chronic pain experienced less pain intensity and decreased levels of disability and depression when they began to serve as peer volunteers for others who also suffered from chronic pain. And individuals who volunteered after recovering from a heart attack reported a reduction in despair and depression and a greater sense of purpose in their lives.[5]

Interestingly—while volunteers in general reported positive mental and physical benefits from helping others—older volunteers were found to experience a greater sense of life satisfaction and greater positive changes in their perceived health than younger volunteers.[6] Researchers speculate that this may be because younger people who help out might feel some sense of obligation that is linked to their other responsibilities, like parenting, whereas older helpers have more discretion in how and whom they choose to help. In Rose's family, volunteering crosses generational lines.

ROSE'S STORY

I guess you'd call us a Boy Scout family. My husband, Dave, achieved the highest rank—Eagle Scout—when he was in his teens, so he was thrilled when all three of our sons showed an interest in scouting. Dave was a troop leader, and I helped out too. Dave and I had full-time jobs, and it wasn't always easy balancing work with all the kids' activities—camping trips, meetings, service projects and the like—and, quite honestly, sometimes it felt more "have to" than "want to." But it was such a great way to be involved in their lives and to get to know their friends and their friends' parents. Now our kids are grown up and have their

*own kids, so we have another generation of scouts—both boys
and girls. Dave and I often get recruited to help, and we love
having this thread of connection with our kids and grandkids.
We go to cookouts, carol with them at nursing homes, serve meals
at homeless shelters, even help sew badges on uniforms. I think
organizations like this are a good vehicle for teaching kids the
importance of service to others. It's great to see them so involved
in the community.*

Although an increasing body of research gives us evidence of
the positive, mental, psychological, and social benefits that caring
for others can provide, I don't think we need studies to convince us
how good we can feel when we help another person. And as Rose
points out, sometimes the benefits trickle down, solidifying family
connections as we connect with others in our community. Before I
began writing this book, I brainstormed my own list of benefits that
caregiving can offer. Here, in no particular order, is my off the-top-
of-my-head list. To me, caregiving

- is an opportunity to practice empathy and compassion
- is a chance to redefine, improve, and evolve relationships,
  making them more honest, open, and deeper
- is an opportunity to exercise and rediscover the better parts
  of ourselves
- is a chance to practice flexibility
- offers the freedom to change lifestyles, perceptions, expectations, judgments, etc.
- is an opportunity to practice life skills like living sanely and
  serenely
- is an opportunity to give back
- is a chance to practice and appreciate the present moment

- is a way to get us "out of our own heads"—lessening worry and depression
- if we're in a Twelve Step program, is a chance to practice the Twelfth Step—the "service Step" (more about this later)
- is a chance to develop new and more intimate connections
- is a reason to get out and get moving
- provides a chance to improve communication skills
- offers the opportunity to expand or discover community (e.g., mutual caregivers, others in the same situation, the community surrounding the person for whom we are helping)
- is a chance to practice reaching out, asking for, and accepting help
- is a possible time of rediscovery/recovery/reconnection
- is an opportunity to practice "delegation" skills
- is an opportunity to use teachable moments with kids (more about this later)
- can help us learn or hone different practical skills (e.g., cooking, home repair, navigating a computer or smartphone)
- is a way to put our values into action
- is a way to expand our own caring circle for times when we might need help
- is an opportunity to connect with and learn from individuals of different ages, ethnicities, cultures, beliefs, and experiences

Take a minute to review my list. What benefits would you add? Many people like Alex from chapter 1 told me how helping others is a way to give back. Individuals like Linda who have been helped in hard times and others who survived trauma and serious illness have also told me how being of service is a way to express gratitude.

LINDA'S STORY

Years ago, when I was a single mom, I got laid off from work and had to get help from community social service programs. I can still remember how embarrassed I was the first time I had to use food stamps and how hard it was to accept help from friends or shop at used clothes stores for clothes for my kids. But I was so grateful to have that help.

I try never to forget what those years were like, and now I volunteer twice a month at a local community service organization that provides food, clothing, school supplies, transportation, and other assistance to residents in need. I love interacting with the folks who come in for help, and I try my best to put them at ease when I sense that same sense of embarrassment I felt so deeply when I was in their shoes. My favorite thing is helping families choose toys for their children at the holidays. The place is decorated so beautifully, and it's so gratifying to watch a mother's or father's delight when they find exactly what they had in mind for their kids.

As these stories and the above list show, when we have opportunities to practice healthy and balanced caregiving, the rewards we gain can be plentiful. However, when our caring lives get out of balance and we find ourselves—sometimes out of habit, sometimes out of necessity—being more care*taker* than care*giver*, many of the above positives can disappear.

When Caring Consumes Us

If you take a moment to look at the chart of common characteristics of both care*takers* and care*givers* in chapter 1 (see pages 16–18 or appendix C), you'll notice how many of the behaviors of caretakers stem from a deep personal need to be in control, accepted, and loved. As has been emphasized throughout, these aren't either/or behaviors or responses. Most of us like to take charge once in a while, and who doesn't want to be accepted and liked? It's when these needs overtake us to the point where most everything we do is "other directed" that things get a bit (or a lot) out of control. That's why so much space in this book has already been devoted to the importance of having more realistic expectations and healthy balance and boundaries.

But all I have to do is page through the many journals I've kept over the years to see how easy it is to throw my good balance and boundary intentions out the window or how often I squash or neglect my own needs or desires because I'm focusing on someone else. So many of my entries begin with something like "Well, all my vows to exercise (or meditate or write or finish a project or fill in the blank) went by the wayside." This admission is often followed with a description of what is happening in *someone else's life*—my concern over someone's health; my sadness over someone else's loss; my worry about a friend who is depressed or sad or facing some challenge. Sometimes my concerns are global, and I go on and on for paragraphs about my fears about the division in our country or the latest world tragedy. I know from my discussions with others that I'm not alone in these feelings. Terry is a case in point.

TERRY'S STORY

I really do enjoy doing favors for friends and relatives and volunteering when I can—so much so that I have trouble saying no or finding time for myself. But I'm getting better at recognizing when I've reached my "compassion quota" and need to pull back a little. One sign is when I find myself yelling at the television when some idiot politician does or says something stupid, or I start crying easily or having disturbing dreams after I've read or heard about something sad in the news—like hearing about a plane crash or something awful happening to a child. I'm always pretty tender-hearted, but when I start feeling like nothing is going right anywhere with anyone—friend and stranger alike—I

need to turn off the television, stop reading the paper for a while,
and start concentrating on taking better care of myself.

In the introduction, I shared a popular joke about knowing you're codependent when you have a near-death experience and someone else's life flashes before your eyes. As my journals attest, we don't have to be at the point of death or crisis to let our lives take a backseat to the lives of others. So often I will wake up and, instead of ticking things off my own to-do list, I'll begin my day by thinking, "I should check in on X to see how her mom is doing; I wonder how Y's weekend was?" It's not that I think it's wrong or abnormal to have these thoughts. I love the people in my life, and my concern about them and my desire to show my support is genuine. But, as I said in my discussion of terms at the beginning of this book, when caring tendencies become extreme or automatic, we risk losing ourselves in the shadows of others. When this happens to me, I know that I'm more on the *caretaker* side of our chart than on the *caregiver* side and, like Terry, need to work at getting things more in balance.

Truth be told, it's *me*—not someone else—who most often tips the scale to the side of *caretaking*. And, if I am to be brutally honest, I know that all too often my obsession with the lives and concerns of others is a way to procrastinate and avoid concentrating on my own stuff. (It's one thing to call a sick friend to see how they're doing—It's quite another to spend an hour or two researching an appliance or car purchase for them, even though they didn't ask or expect me to do this!) As a writer, I often find it so much easier to rush to the aid and support of others than to face a blank page. As a person who has never been an avid exerciser, I find calling to check in on a friend far more inviting than going to the gym. (I never remember I could "kill two birds" by asking them to take a walk with me instead of chatting on the phone.) And concentrating on others and anticipating their needs can feel so noble! But when I reach my caregiving limits—a threshold that differs for each of us—it's as if a huge neon "TILT" sign lights up, letting me know something is out of balance. Here's how Mark describes this tendency.

MARK'S STORY

I remember a long-ago Sunday school teacher talking about how the Bible says, "I am third" (meaning after God and my neighbor). My sad joke on myself is that for a long time I didn't even think I was third—I was last. Growing up, I got the message that my opinion was not welcome and never valued; that I was never right. I was carefully taught that my own needs weren't as important as other people's, so I learned early on that doing for others was all that mattered and that concentrating on my own needs was selfish. This has gotten in my way over the years in being there for others without feeling somewhat resentful. Balancing self with others can still be a tug-of-war sometimes, and I have to work to get past those old feelings. But when I do (thanks in large part to the support and encouragement I get from my partner), I find great satisfaction and joy from helping others because I'm doing it out of a spirit of love and generosity instead of obligation.

Sometimes it's our bodies that signal a warning that we're reaching the imbalance Mark described. When I feel overwhelmed by worrying about someone or trying to do too much for too many too often, to the point that I'm not tending to my own personal or work life the way I should, I'll often get a headache or feel frazzled or depressed. Sometimes I can actually feel my blood pressure rising—a feeling that is confirmed when I measure it and find that it's much higher than normal.

If caring responses to ordinary life events can get to a point where we are affected both emotionally and physically, imagine the toll that caring for someone with a serious or ongoing care need can take on a primary caregiver. While healthy and balanced caregiving can lengthen our lives and improve our health, primary caregivers in difficult and challenging circumstances face serious threats to their health and well-being. Research shows that overwhelmed caregivers have a greater chance of dying sooner than their non-caregiving peers. Some caregivers who repeatedly neglect their own physical and mental health even risk dying before the person they are caring for. As Susan Toth cautions in the book I previously mentioned called *No Saints around Here,* "A caregiver needs to make plans, but she should always make them in disappearing ink." In a chapter called "Failing Battery," she writes:

> Yesterday morning, remembering that my aide Martha would soon come for several hours, I thought, "Hey! After I've driven to the grocery store, the bank, and the mall to order new bifocals, I might still have time for a quick walk." In deciding how I could apportion my time, I had, as usual, in George W. Bush's famous coinage, "mis-underestimated."[7]

She goes on to relate how on her way to the grocery store, her car developed mysterious electrical problems. Because her mechanic couldn't get her in for an hour, she rushed to the store, where she found the lines longer than usual. Picking out new frames took more time than she calculated, because "caregiver or not, I still have regrettable vanity." Then she got a chatty teller at the bank. She finally made it to the auto garage, where she was relieved to find there was no serious problem with her car. She was amused when her favorite mechanic gave her the news, "Your battery is marginal." She wrote:

> My battery was marginal. I thought about that. I thought about it all the way home. I was quite tired now. I wouldn't have time for a walk. I wished I could take a nap. Yes . . . my battery is definitely marginal.[8]

Because primary caregivers devote so much necessary time and attention to the care needs of a loved one, they often don't get the sleep or exercise they need. They frequently eat poorly, don't take care of themselves when they are ill, or put their own medical needs on hold as they schedule appointments and manage medicines for the person they are taking care of. This can cause them to become exhausted and overly stressed.

While stress can play an important role in our lives by keeping us alert when we face threats like stopping a child from running into the street, or focused when we need to be sharp in a tension-filled situation, extreme or chronic stress can lead to serious problems. You might say that normal stress is a large ripple in a stream; extreme stress is a tsunami. When a perceived threat has passed, our body's alarm system turns off and our stress levels usually return to normal. With extreme stress over time, our bodies won't necessarily completely recoup, and our health can be seriously compromised.

But it isn't just primary caregivers who can get stressed out. When our lives are out of balance, we all can be adversely affected by stress. Like most things related to caregiving, what we can handle differs from person to person and situation to situation. Some of us are expert at juggling a number of demands at once; some of us like Alex (our friend from chapter 1) even thrive on such challenges. Others of us are better at handling one thing at a time and can easily get stressed when caring concerns and tasks seem to come at us from all directions. Still others are energized and razor sharp and superbly competent when a crisis hits, then feel fatigued or stressed when things settle down and our emotions catch up with us.

I know from personal experience and from the stories of others how demanding and stress-laden being the primary caregiver for a loved one who requires an extra level of care can be. But as I mentioned, I've also found that even casual caregiving can take a toll if we stretch ourselves too thin doing too much for others and not enough for ourselves. We may not feel the same degree of exhaustion or stress as a primary caregiver, but, as Nancy explains, if this imbalance goes unchecked, we can still experience stress-related physical and mental repercussions.

NANCY'S STORY

I have to work very hard not to put others' needs before my own. I am learning that I need to set boundaries for what I need and can do and will enjoy—not always give priority to what I'm guessing someone else needs or would enjoy. I know I need to entertain less, work less, rest more, and take better care of myself. But it's challenging because I have such high standards for my home, for the kind of friend, parent, wife, and grandparent I have been and want to continue to be.

I'm a terrible sleeper by nature, and I'm worse when I'm stressed or worried. Our daughter was seriously ill for the better part of a year. I was so anxious about her and her husband and kids that I couldn't unclutter my brain when I went to bed, no matter how tired I was. I tried my usual "fixes," like using guided meditation tapes, getting massages, and exercising when I could, but nothing seemed to work. Over-the-counter sleep aids didn't work either. I just felt like electricity was always running through my veins, and I got heart palpitations. No matter what I did, I always felt edgy. I wanted to be there for my daughter and kids and be available to help her husband, but I was no good to anybody the way I felt. So I finally went to a doctor for my anxiety, and she prescribed a mild antidepressant. That made such a difference.

The Signs and Symptoms of Stress

Left untended, long-term stress can lead to serious health problems, like ongoing high blood pressure, a suppressed immune system, an increased risk of heart attack and stroke, severe headaches, or sleep problems. It can also lead to eating disorders, depression, or addiction problems.

Caregivers who experience a number of the following signs and symptoms risk stress overload:

Cognitive Symptoms

Memory problems

Inability to concentrate

Poor judgment

Seeing only the negative

Anxious or racing thoughts

Constant worrying

Physical Symptoms

Aches and pains

Diarrhea or constipation

Nausea, dizziness

Chest pain, rapid heartbeat

Frequent colds

Emotional Symptoms

Moodiness

Irritability or short temper

Agitation, inability to relax

Feeling overwhelmed

Sense of loneliness or isolation

General unhappiness

Behavioral Symptoms

Eating too much or too little

Sleeping too much or too little

Isolating yourself from others

Using alcohol, cigarettes,

    or drugs to relax

Nervous habits like nail biting

Take a moment to review these symptoms of stress. Have you or someone you know experienced any of these when caring for others? How many are you or they experiencing now?

Stress is like the tension on a guitar string. If the string is turned too tightly, it snaps; if it is strung too loosely, it is limp and sounds dull. Again it comes down to balance. A little stress can keep us at the ready. When stress throws our lives out of balance, however, our "inner strings" can stretch to the breaking point or go limp, leaving us feeling depleted or even depressed.

The longer we ignore stress symptoms, the more serious they can become. If you are consistently experiencing a number of the above symptoms, it might be a good idea to consult a qualified medical professional, as Nancy did. As we'll see, asking for and accepting help is an important element of self-care.

Stress Management and Self-Care

I want to start this section by stating with emphasis, SELF-CARE IS *NOT* SELFISH! If this were an audio book, I'd shout that reminder out to all of you compassionate beings out there who are reading these words. You may have heard the oxygen mask example that is often used to illustrate the importance of self-care—the one that talks about how flight attendants always instruct airline passengers that if an emergency occurs, they should remember to put on their own masks first before they help others. This comparison is popular because it's a perfect reminder that we're of little use to others if we can't breathe. Self-care allows us to inhale—it is the second wind we need to muster up the strength and energy to care for others with a clear mind and open heart.

Even though deep in our open hearts we know this is true, for overburdened caregivers or caretakers who have grown used to charting their lives by other people's compasses, the reminder to eat better, exercise, rest, and meditate can seem like just one more thing to add to our already too-long to-do list. I know that when I'm feeling overwhelmed and stressed, the last thing I want to see is some perky little model on television telling me how a bubble bath or flavored coffee can "take me away." "Like I have time for a bath!" I want to scream at them, not realizing that if I weren't watching television, maybe I *would* have time for a bath.

At its best, self-care is a holistic endeavor in which we tend to our bodies, our minds, and our spirits. Before we discuss some self-care challenges and suggestions, I urge you to take a moment to take your current physical, emotional, and mental "pulse." Jot down your honest answers to the following questions to see how well you are currently taking care of yourself:

- Are you honoring your body? Have you listened to its aches, tensions, and feelings? Have you been taking time to rest when you were tired? Have you gotten some exercise? Are you eating balanced and healthy meals?

- Are you honoring your mind? Have you taken the time to read a good book, take an interesting class, or learn something new? Have you been able to exchange ideas and talk about opinions with a friend?

- Are you honoring your emotions? Have you been able to express your feelings in your journal or to another person? Have you spent quality time with someone this week? Have you taken time to play and laugh? Have you given yourself time to cry when and if you needed to?

- Are you honoring your spirit and soul? Have you spent time in prayer, meditation, or solitary thought? Have you taken the time to be quiet with yourself and with nature? Have you read something inspirational or listened to beautiful music?

This checklist is not meant to nag or scold. So try not to despair if you, like so very many of us, haven't been taking the best care of yourself. Think of it as a gentle nudge—a way to take your self-care temperature from time to time. We often use this list in our caregiver group as a way to check in and as a reminder for all of us to pause, slow down, and inhale before we go on to meet the busy demands of life in general and lives as caregivers in particular.

Obstacles to Self-Care: A Brief Review

Many of the care*taker* characteristics we've discussed in previous pages can also be seen as behaviors that can interfere with caring for ourselves while we're caring for others. The chart on the next page lists some of these characteristics seen through the lens of self-care, together with a suggested remedy that might open the door to better self-care.

As you may notice when you read through self-care obstacles and remedies listed in this chart, just about everything we've discussed so far ultimately directs us to the importance of self-care in caregiving. If, when reading through the list, you have that "Ouch; this still strikes a chord" reaction to one of the obstacles or suggested remedies, I encourage you to revisit the relevant sections in preceding chapters for a more detailed discussion of that issue or issues before

Possible Obstacle to Self-Care	Suggested Remedy
Needing to be the "special one" (defining our worth by how we think others need us) leaves little time for reflection and self-care.	Finding our appropriate place in a circle of care helps us share care responsibilities with someone else in our "ring," which gives us more time for self-care.
Wanting to be the perfect caregiver can lead to doing too much "other care" and not enough self-care.	Embracing our imperfection leaves room for self-care and helps prevent a "one-up/one-down" relationship.
Having unreal or unmet expectations can lead to disappointment, depression, and poor self-care.	Accepting what we cannot change and watching out for the "if only," "should," or "always/never" messages we send ourselves can reduce stress and resentment, increasing our ability to care for others as we care for ourselves.
Believing messages about the "duty" of caregiving and the importance of others can discourage us from caring for ourselves because we were taught it is selfish to tend to our own needs before we help others.	Sifting through *both* positive and negative caregiving messages for those who serve us well can lead to more compassionate caregiving and a healthier approach to self-care.
Having inappropriate boundaries can turn a casual offer of help into an all-consuming care situation, leaving little time for self-care.	Setting and maintaining healthy boundaries helps us better assess a caregiving commitment to see what areas of *our* lives could be adversely affected.
Having "unboundaried" empathy can cause us to get so consumed and tangled up with someone's problems and feelings that we get adversely affected (e.g., stressed or depressed), which can put our well-being and self-care at risk.	"Emptying our own cup" beforehand helps us establish appropriate boundaries so we can be fully present and more aware of a traumatized person's emotions versus our reactions to *their* story, which helps us take better care of ourselves in emotionally challenging caregiving situations.

we move on and go deeper into the subject of self-care. (I have also included a copy of this chart at the back of this book, labeled appendix E, and I encourage you to keep a copy of it on hand for those times when you may feel in need of a "self-care booster shot.")

Having Compassion for Ourselves

I believe that self-compassion begets self-care. Kristin Neff, a psychology professor and a well-known expert on the subject, describes self-compassion as "giving ourselves the same kindness and care we'd give a good friend."[9] She writes that

> Instead of mercilessly judging and criticizing yourself for various inadequacies or shortcomings, self-compassion means you are kind and understanding when confronted with personal failings—after all, who said you were supposed to be perfect?[10]

Neff stresses that self-compassion is *not* the same as self-esteem, which is about our feelings of self-worth. While low self-esteem can lead to self-doubt and depression, Neff points out how our culture's emphasis on the importance of high self-esteem can cause us to be self-absorbed or think we need to be special in order to feel good about ourselves. With self-compassion, she says, "You don't have to feel better than others to feel good about yourself. Self-compassion also allows for greater self-clarity because personal failings can be acknowledged with kindness and do not have to be hidden."[11]

For care*takers*, the idea of showing ourselves the same patience, empathetic compassion, acceptance, and support is probably a revolutionary one. While we might be nonjudgmental of others, so many of us are our own harshest and most unforgiving critics. When we're in a self-critical frame of mind, it is very easy to convince ourselves that we are not worthy of self-care.

Quieting the Critic Within

In a long-ago writing class, I learned a useful exercise for a way to interrupt the stream of negative and distorted thoughts that often run through our minds when we feel in conflict, in despair, or overcome with self-doubt. I found it so helpful that I've shared it with my creative writing students and incorporated it in my own writing.

The idea is to have a dialogue on the page with our internal critic—that little guy who sits on our shoulder hissing in our ear about how worthless we are. First we let him talk, and then we respond. I found this exercise to be a great self-compassion builder, and I urge those of you who have a tendency to be overly hard on yourselves to try it.

One of my conversations might go like this:

Critical self: "I feel like such a lousy friend and daughter."

Compassionate self: "You do lots of things right. Just today you remembered to send your mom a card, you met a deadline, checked in on M., and helped an elderly woman find her car."

Critical self: "But I never seem to be able to keep up with it all. I'm tired and my house is always a mess. All my friends seem able to exercise, work, and keep their houses immaculate."

Compassionate self: "You were up late working and got up early to put a load of laundry in and do dishes before you left. Maybe you can find time for a nap or a walk later. I think your friends feel overwhelmed too. Don't you remember S. telling you how she threw all her clutter in her closet when the doorbell rang?"

Critical self: "I planned to get things done around the house tonight, but told L. I'd meet her for dinner."

Compassionate self: "That sounds relaxing and fun, and you've been missing her. Maybe she'd like to walk around the lake before you go out. Would you rather be cleaning?"

Critical self: "No, you're right. It's supposed to be a gorgeous night, and it's rare that we can find time to be together. Housework can wait."

Well, you get the idea. When I have these conversations with myself, my distorted thoughts are usually quieted by my softer and more supportive self. I've also dialogued with another person in my journal when I've been hurt or confused about a tension-filled interaction. I let my friend "speak" to me on the page and, more often than not, I emerge feeling kinder and more understanding. I've even had a "conversation" with my dead grandmother, asking for her wise counsel and imagining her responses. Of course, it is really me who holds the answers, but these dialogues help me correct my perspective and gain a clearer understanding of others in the process. They are a way to practice empathy for myself and others, which allows me to be more care*giver* than care*taker*.

What kind of messages do you give yourself? Are you being as kind with yourself as you are with others? Alice discovered that being more self-compassionate helped her feel more deserving of self-care.

ALICE'S STORY

Like so many caregivers, I always used to feel that it was selfish of me if I put myself or my needs before the needs of others. I'm an artist, and when I don't have time to paint, I often get sad and depressed. But I'm a sucker when people ask me for favors. For example, a disabled artist friend asked me to take her to a class we both signed up for. I gave her rides and carried her supplies, which involved lugging them up to the second floor. The classes were from 10 a.m. to 4 p.m., and if she was in pain and needed to go home, it meant we both had to leave early. I paid a lot of money to take the class and I enjoyed it so much, so I found myself getting irritated and resentful when this happened. This used to happen at my house too. Sometimes other artist friends would come over wanting to paint with me, but I spent so much time teaching them something they wanted to learn, I hardly ever got to work on my own things.

Thankfully, with the help of a supportive therapist, I learned that I mattered too; that I could choose when I wanted to work on my own art and when I wanted to be with others. I've always loved to paint, and I've had many successes along the way. She convinced me that carving out time for myself and my art was a way to respect myself and honor the gift I'd been given. Now I don't feel guilty when I take time for myself. I learned I can choose when I want to do a favor for someone. And when I do, my attitude has shifted dramatically. It actually feels good to help because I'm doing it for the right reason.

Take Time to Make Time

If you made a list of all the things you intend to do today, would anything having to do with self-care be on it? Part of having self-compassion is convincing ourselves that we need (and are entitled to) time for ourselves. As Alice described in her story, when we are used to putting other people's needs before our own, it is all too easy for our best intentions to go by the wayside. Just think about how much time you devote to the care and concerns of others. Now think of how much time you spend on caring for yourself. If things lean too much toward the caregiving side, you may want to examine your priorities to make sure your agenda is truly your agenda.

Pause for a moment and jot down the answers to the following questions:

- What do I need to accomplish today?
- What do I need or want to do for myself today?
- What do I want to do for or with others today?
- How will I go about accomplishing what I need and want to get done?
- How will I allow room for flexibility?

Of course there will be times when life, with all its surprises and challenges, will get in the way of our best intentions. When that happens, it helps to remind ourselves that these are just detours; we don't have to abandon all plans of self-care and can make adjustments. Even a ten-minute walk is better than no walk. If we treat our "self time" as sacred, maybe even writing it down in bold letters on the family calendar, we just might begin to believe that we deserve rest, relaxation, and play.

Most time-management articles mention the importance of prioritizing and organizing. Here are some tips I've come across that you may want to consider:

- Make written lists of the things or activities you need to do in order of priority, and cross off each as you accomplish it. If possible, try to group errands and appointments so you can consolidate trips.

- Plan ahead by setting aside a particular day on which to pay bills, grocery shop, do laundry and other household chores, and so on. Remember that the Internet can be your friend when it comes to researching the closest store or best deal, but also remember that it can be your downfall when you open your computer and discover you've lost over an hour reading emails or Facebook.

- Check your calendar ahead of time, and buy all birthday and anniversary cards a few months in advance. Have a good stock of note, sympathy, congratulations, and thank-you cards and stamps on hand so you don't have to make a special trip to the store each time an occasion arises. One of my best investments was a calendar notebook that has a page with pockets for cards and a line for each day of the month. When I see the perfect birthday card for someone, I slip it into the appropriate pocket and I'm all set when the day rolls around. That is, if I can remember to check the notebook!

- Try not to overcommit. Give yourself permission to politely refuse invitations or requests for favors, to say yes with conditions, or to change your mind even when you have said yes. Circumstances and feelings can change, and you may be feeling too exhausted or stressed to enjoy a party or be able to help a friend.

- Remember to actually schedule time for yourself so you can take a walk, listen to music, read, relax, exercise or do something fun with a friend or by yourself. Exercise is a great way to recharge our batteries because it helps us sleep better, reduces tension and depression, and increases our energy level and alertness. To carve out more time for yourself, consider bartering child care if you have kids. If you are a primary caregiver, try to find respite care when you need a break or ask a friend if they could sit or visit your loved one, as Denise did.

DENISE'S STORY

When my husband was laid up for several months, his best friend came over every Sunday so I could go to church and continue to sing in the choir. He told me it gave him the chance to have some "guy time." It was great because his wife, a good friend of mine, sang in the choir with me so we got to spend time together too. Sometimes we went out for brunch or got a nice walk in after church. When I'd come home, I'd often find small repair jobs finished. I never had to ask for these things to be done, and I know it was a relief to my husband that I didn't have to handle everything by myself.

Asking for and Accepting Help

When I asked overstressed caregivers what they thought the hardest thing was about caring for others, many would mention the difficulty of asking for and accepting help—a common malady for those who are more comfortable doing for others than having things done for them. Admitting that we can't be everything for everyone is a sign of self-awareness, and accepting help when it is offered is a way to show ourselves the compassion we are so ready to give to others. When we accept help, we give ourselves permission to be vulnerable and can let go of our perfectionism. When we practice the give-and-take that comes with doing and accepting favors, we often discover that our relationships can feel more balanced. Care receivers who have been helped repeatedly by a friend have told me how good it feels to be able to do something for that person in return. Many call it a true gift. However, as Charlotte relates, that doesn't mean it's easy for independent caregivers *or* receivers to ask for assistance.

CHARLOTTE'S STORY

I've given care and I've been cared for, so I've been on both sides of the caring coin, so to speak. I've discovered that the hardest thing about asking for help is asking. I don't think it ceases to feel like an imposition, even when saints like my husband or our friends provide compelling evidence that when they say "anything," they mean it. That includes granting requests for help and doing favors. But it's still a little humiliating to have to ask a dear one to do something very unpleasant and intimate when you are feeling vulnerable and totally dependent.

Sometimes the process is easier if we can break it down. First, it helps to be clear about the need or problem. Next, it helps to identify who can most appropriately give you the help you need. If you filled out your list of people you could call in various situations that we discussed in chapter 4, you're already ahead of the game. Because we, of course, can't anticipate what responses we'll receive or know if a person will be available, it's a good idea to have more than one option or person in mind.

The last step is to actually ask for the help you need. It helps to be as clear and specific in your request as you can be and, if possible, estimate the amount of time you think such a favor may require. If someone is unable to help you, try your best to accept their answer at face value. Thank that person and ask the next person on your list or ask if they have an idea of whom else you might contact. If they seem hesitant or uncertain if they will be available, you can simply suggest they just think about it and get back to you. Those who cannot help today might be more than willing to help tomorrow.

Compassion Fatigue

Without healthy boundaries and good self-care, overburdened caregivers are at risk for compassion fatigue, which is just what it sounds like. Just as self-care can benefit body, mind, and spirit, compassion fatigue can negatively affect our entire being, causing us to become mentally, physically, and spiritually exhausted. Those who suffer from compassion fatigue, which some call "caregiving shutdown," can become withdrawn and joyless, irritable, depressed, uninterested in intimacy or sex, and feel like they're just going through the motions of life instead of living it to its fullest. Here's how Stuart and Charles described their own compassion fatigue.

STUART'S STORY

Because my partner has such a good attitude and is so easy to care for, the main problems are with me. He gets very confused, so it falls on me to handle our schedule, make his appointments, pay the bills, etc. I get exhausted and easily frustrated because I forget he is no longer capable of doing the things he used to be able to do. (He is very clever at covering up many problems, so he often "fakes" it very well.) I've found that my frustration and fatigue often lead to irritability, which adds guilt into the equation— because I know he would help more if he were only able.

CHARLES'S STORY

It was very difficult to balance my responsibilities as a husband and father with taking care of my mom. The time came when I felt like caring for her became my life. I lived an hour away at the time, so I'd drive to her house early every morning to take care of whatever she needed or do things around the house that needed

to be taken care of. Then I'd go to the office to try to work as long
as I could, then back to her house to take her to her appointments
or do chores or errands or whatever else needed to be done. Then
I'd drive back home. I rarely saw my wife or kids during that time,
which was hard on all of us. When I did have rare time at home,
I was just too tired or down to go anywhere or do anything with
them.

Review the signs and symptoms of stress overload listed in this chapter. If you are feeling the effects of too much stress and compassion fatigue, it is important that you seek help from a qualified medical or mental health care provider.

Summing It Up

One Wednesday, a friend emailed a meme that said, "This is your midweek reminder. Relax! You have enough. You do enough. You are enough." Perhaps we should all reproduce these words on an 8½ by 11-inch piece of paper and hang it next to our bathroom mirrors as a reminder each day to slow down and take care.

As we've discussed, self-care is not just a gift we give ourselves. When we maintain healthy boundaries, practice self-compassion, educate ourselves about the warning signs of stress, and practice the other elements of self-care covered in this chapter, we have a better chance of giving compassionate care to others without risking our own health and well-being.

Self-care is a prevention tool that helps us more effectively meet caregiving opportunities and challenges with self-awareness and intention. Julie Beck, the writer quoted at the beginning of this chapter who compared the lack of self-care to being in a thunderstorm without an umbrella, closed the article from which her words were taken by saying, "The chaos swirls out there, and you eventually have to wade back into it. But if you stop by the self-care café, on your way out, you can grab an umbrella to take with you into the storm."[12]

Self-care is shelter from the storms of life that may come our way or strike our loved ones. Practicing good self-care *all* the time better prepares us for the particularly difficult caregiving situations that will be discussed in the next chapter. We'll also talk more about the extreme importance of caring for ourselves in these circumstances and explore ways to expand our own circle of support.

CHAPTER 7

When "Lightning" Strikes

Preparing for the Unexpected

I'm reminded that the Chinese ideogram for danger also means opportunity. This is not to suggest that we seek out danger, but that we look for the openings, when broken by experience, by which we can find our connection to the un-seeable stream we often forget we are a part of.

Perhaps the purpose of crisis, if there is one, is not to break us as much as to break us open.

—MARK NEPO, *THE BOOK OF AWAKENINGS*[1]

In the best of circumstances, caregivers can choose when they want to lend a helping hand or an attentive ear. But often—sometimes when we're least expecting it—an emergency arises, and we are called into immediate action. The phone awakens you in the middle of the night, and fear clutches your heart as your mind races with thoughts of "What has happened? Who is hurt? Did someone die?" The school calls, telling you, "Not to worry, but your son was injured at football practice and we'd like you to meet us at the hospital." Or a friend calls sobbing, with news of a frightening medical test result. Sometimes it is you who makes that call. Here's what happened to my friends April and Craig.

APRIL'S STORY

Craig and I are what I guess you'd call "loving friends." We used to date, and we care about each other deeply, but we both agreed ours was not a "forever-after"/marriage kind of partnership. We were in the habit of checking in with each other several times a week, and one morning I called him after I got to work. I got alarmed because he sounded so strange—his speech was slurred and he wasn't making sense. He didn't drink or use drugs, so I immediately knew something was terribly wrong and called 911. He was having a stroke!

Although many of his physical and cognitive functions have returned, the stroke affected him permanently, so he is unable to care for himself. His elderly sister is infirm and doesn't live here, and since I'm not his wife, this has all been so tough. Luckily, we both have a circle of terrific friends who have helped out in so many ways.

As April experienced, the longer we live, the more curveballs life seems to throw us. Our parents age, our kids grow up, our bodies change. Most of these changes are normal and gradual, and we can usually handle them in stride. On good days, we might even joke about our occasional aches and pains, laugh about becoming forgetful, and be able to stay open to the joy and surprises that may come our way. But there are also those times when, as the poet William Wordsworth wrote long ago, "The world is too much with us," and it seems like disaster and disease lurk behind every corner. One day everything is fine, and the next morning a close friend has a stroke, or we find out a parent's "eccentric" behavior is really Alzheimer's.

When caregiving chooses us, it's more important than ever to have our "caring house" in order, to have our list of resources as well as our circle of care in place, to sharpen our empathy and listening skills when we can, and to regularly practice the elements of self-care we've discussed throughout the preceding pages. While it's impossible to anticipate all the caregiving trials that may come our way, this chapter deals with some of the more difficult challenges compassionate caregivers have faced and discusses how they handled such situations.

When "Lightning" Strikes

Lightning is the word that came to mind when I thought about all the people I have had the honor to meet and interview over the years whose lives were interrupted by unexpected trauma and challenges. One of them, Mary Peek, used it in the title of her book, *The Awful Lightning*, to describe such a life-altering event.

Mary was a forty-seven-year-old schoolteacher on August 22, 1970, when a homemade bomb exploded in a restroom wastebasket at a St. Paul department store while she was combing her hair on her way to a luncheon date with her husband. She almost died. The bomb caused serious and permanent shrapnel injuries that required her to walk with a cane the rest of her life. Her hearing was also shattered, and her lungs were scorched, causing a chronic pulmonary disease that ultimately led to her death in 2005. This bomb went off during a time of extreme civil unrest in this country and was planted by a fifteen-year-old—a boy who at the time was the same age as Mary's youngest son, Tom.

I've learned a lot about compassionate caring from this remarkable family, and I share their story in these pages because I think it so beautifully illustrates what Mark Nepo expressed in the epigraph to this chapter when he wrote how crisis can either break us or connect us to that "un-seeable stream we often forget we are a part of." Here's how Tom described this phenomenon:

> My family might have become embittered. . . . But our mother, who'd spent years working for social justice and peace, guided us to a deeper, more constructive understanding of the political violence that maimed her. She knew that the bomber—son of a civil rights activist—was too young and wrathful to understand

that progress requires not anger, but inner strength, patience
and unfailing persistence.[2]

Mary not only modeled these virtues for her family, she also
demonstrated what it means to be a compassionate caregiver. In
addition to her many other contributions, she used her experience
with and knowledge of trauma to support others who, like my husband, struggle with PTSD. We will be forever grateful for the role
she played in getting him the professional help he needed when
lightning struck our own family.

I know all too well that my friend Mary set the caregiving/care-
receiving bar higher than most of us could hope to reach. Of course,
she didn't immediately leap from crisis to compassion. Her physical
and emotional scars were deep, and the journey was a long and
tough one for her and her entire family. But just knowing that care
and kindheartedness can exist and even grow stronger in the wake
of such adversity gives me great hope and something to strive for.
And more to the point of this book, as a teacher and community activist, she had tools and a support system already in place when her
"awful lightning" struck. So did her devoted husband and primary
caregiver, a respected and well-connected psychologist and activist
who received many awards for his work on mental health reform in
the State of Minnesota.

Although their story is extraordinary, it is one of many: Every
day, in every way, someone is called upon to help when they're least
expecting it. Caring tools and practices are like car or home emergency kits. While we can't stop the storms of life from coming, we
can at least know what to do and where to turn first if we have our
"kits" at the ready when these storms do roll in.

First Things First

It has been a helpful exercise to imagine what an actual caregiver/
care receiver "emergency kit" might contain. I started thinking of
family and friends who have been alone when they had bike or car
accidents, falls, or other emergencies. I thought of how my dad

didn't know where to find my phone number when Mom had a stroke; how friends were knocked unconscious when one fell on an icy driveway and the other got thrown riding his horse. Perhaps many of you already carry ICE (In Case of Emergency) cards in your wallets, but what about those times when you may not have your wallets with you?

This is the question I posed to my husband the other day when he was heading out the door to go for a bike ride. It was one of those aha moments. He doesn't carry his wallet when he bikes, so he took the time to make copies of his wallet info for his bike bag, his gym bag, and the fanny pack he carries on hikes. Although I am diligent about carrying my own info when I bike or hike, I realized I hadn't updated it or made a copy for my own gym bag. When we talked more about it, we decided it was a good idea as primary caregivers for each other to also carry each other's medical information and— while we were at it—we emailed copies to our daughter and her husband, who are listed as our other emergency contacts in case they should ever have to contact our physicians or gain access to our records.

Following is the emergency and medical information we now carry. I also encourage you to obtain contact numbers and relevant information from those you care for on a regular basis or who may have you listed as an emergency contact person. Knowing where to find relevant information in a hurry can save both a caregiver and a care receiver valuable time. A template for an In Case of Emergency Card is in appendix H; feel free to make copies of it to fill out.

IN CASE OF EMERGENCY (ICE) CARD

Medical emergency information for _____
(I include my name, address, home and cell phone numbers)

Emergency contacts: _____
(I include names and relationships [e.g., spouse, son, etc.] and both home and cell phone numbers)

Insurance information: _____
(I include insurance company name and phone number, and a
note that says "cards in wallet")

Primary physician: _____
(I include name and phone number)

Medical conditions: _____
(I list any ongoing medical problems, e.g., high blood pressure,
asthma, etc.)

Blood type: _____
(e.g., O positive)

Allergies: _____
(I list drug allergies and things like yellow jacket stings)

Medications: _____
(I list both prescription and over-the-counter drugs, like 81 mg
aspirin)

Because my husband and I frequently watch our grandsons, our
daughter also made sure we have the names of their pediatrician
and their insurance information in case an emergency arises when
they are in our care and we cannot immediately reach her or her
husband—a good idea for all of you who care for children. We keep
this information on our refrigerator for quick access.

As Elise discovered, having emergency information readily accessible came in very handy for her as primary caregiver when her
husband had a medical problem away from home and they had to
act quickly.

ELISE'S STORY

*My husband and I were on one of our camping/kayaking adven-
tures when our lives took a dramatic—and permanent—twist.
We had been gone five days when the mild on-and-off stomach*

pain he had been having got worse. It was a beautiful Florida Friday afternoon when we came in from kayaking, and he just didn't look right to me. He was somewhat jaundiced, and he looked like he was in pain. Over his objections, I insisted on trying to get hold of his primary doctor. Luckily, I had cell phone coverage and, as active retirees, we always traveled with our medical information, so I didn't have to scramble for numbers or rely on the Internet. Our doctor called back right away. He alarmed me a little when he said, "I don't like the sounds of what you are describing, and I want you to go to the closest hospital emergency room right away." Fortunately, we weren't that far from our local hospital, so we rushed home, switched out the truck for the car, and went to the hospital. They did tests, discovered a mass in his pancreas, and admitted him.

I also contacted our doctor son who at that time was an administrator at a leading cancer hospital in Milwaukee. He made arrangements for us to be admitted there, so I rushed home to pack for the two of us to fly to Wisconsin the next day. We traveled often, so I had the list of what needed to be done in the house, who to call in such an emergency, and what neighbors to notify to check on things while we were gone. I also knew what to pack on short notice. I was on "hyper drive," so believe me, I could not have done all that without our lists!

The diagnosis was advanced pancreatic cancer. Little did we know that we would be in Milwaukee for weeks until we could return to Florida for his treatment regimen. Our kayaks stayed on our truck for months, and, sadly, we were never able to camp together again because he only lived a year. He died five months after our fiftieth anniversary. I still can't believe how fast life can change. It seems like I was kayaking and laughing with him one moment, and planning his memorial service the next.

Elise's experience underscores how important it is for caregivers to have access to the information they may need—not only in such an emergency, but in more ordinary situations as well. For instance, the HIPAA (Health Insurance Portability & Accountability Act) rules protect an individual's medical information, so it is necessary that the person you are caring for give their medical providers permission for you to talk with them if, indeed, the patient wants you cleared for such discussions. Most doctors' offices will have a consent form available for the patient to sign that is on file (although it may have to be renewed from time to time). At other times—for instance, when a care receiver wants the caregiver who takes them to the doctor to sit in on a medical discussion—verbal consent is usually sufficient because everyone involved is present. The important thing to remember is not to presume you can discuss someone's medical condition with their doctor(s) even if you are their primary caregiver. Elise told me how important it was to have consent forms on file with her husband's doctors, pharmacy, and insurance company. She told me, "It saved hours of frustration or being put on hold—especially on those days when he was too ill or confused to make these calls himself."

Laws and procedures vary from place to place and state to state, and I am not an attorney. But I encourage caregivers and care receivers to find out from a qualified person or resource what documents might be necessary in those cases when someone has to act on behalf of another person regarding both medical and financial matters.

Caregivers as Medical Advocates

According to the Family Caregiver Alliance, about 37 percent of family caregivers administer medications, give injections, and manage medical treatment for the person they care for in addition to taking on household chores, shopping, transportation, and personal care. Of that number, 77 percent of those caregivers frequently need to communicate with physicians about medications, treatments, and other issues.[3]

The Family Caregiver Alliance offers some tips for making such communication and medical visits more efficient, which I've paraphrased and condensed below. They suggest:

- Writing down questions, concerns, and problems ahead of time, such as changes in symptoms, questions about medications, and any concerns you may have about your duties as caregiver.

- Enlisting the help of a nurse who can answer questions about various tests or surgical procedures, or about managing medications at home.

- Trying to schedule the first appointment in the morning or after lunch in order to reduce waiting time, and being clear about the reasons for scheduling such an appointment.

- Calling ahead to see if a doctor is on schedule and reminding the receptionist of the need for your visit when you arrive.

- Taking someone with you as an "extra set of ears" to make it easier to sift through and remember what a doctor or nurse said. My mother always recorded my parents' doctor visits. Their doctor never minded this, and transcribing the recording helped my mom better understand what had been covered at a visit. She would then email her notes to all three of us siblings, so we could also keep up-to-date on their respective health issues.

Keeping Track of It All

So many of the caregivers I know and have interviewed told me how easy it is to get weighed down by the mountain of medical information they have to manage for the person they care for. Keeping track of meds, appointments, and bills, as well as wading through tons of information about test results, diagnoses, treatment plans, surgery options and dates, and the like can be an exhausting and overwhelming aspect of caregiving. More than a few caregivers told me they often felt robbed of precious time with their loved one because so much of their time and energy was consumed by such tasks. As one respondent put it, "I felt more nurse than wife. One day I told my husband, 'I miss you,' and he sadly said, 'I miss me too. I miss us.'"

I still hold the image of my exhausted sister standing by her kitchen counter on which she had placed all her husband's prescription drugs for his Parkinson's disease, cancer, and blood disorder. When I woke up at two in the morning to go to the bathroom, I saw the kitchen light on and found her trying to sort out eighteen bottles of meds. With tears in her eyes, she looked at me wearily and said, "I couldn't sleep, so I thought I'd try a new system to keep everything straight." On an 8½ by 11-inch piece of typing paper, she had placed one of each pill, under which she had written how much he should take and when. "Sinemet, 5/day, 2 @ breakfast, 2 @ lunch, 1 @ supper," "Remeron, 1 @ bed," "OxyContin (12 hr. pain)," "Compazine (nausea)," and so on.

My husband and I had arranged to stay with them for several weeks, and we were very clear about where we fit in the overall circle of care. We were there to care for my sister while she cared for her husband. For some reason I shall never grasp, my husband loves to do spreadsheets, so he took it upon himself to develop one for all our brother-in-law's meds, with columns that listed the prescription, the dose and other instructions, and the possible side effects so they could easily track what pill might be causing what symptom. It simplified things greatly and carved out more time for my sister and her husband to be together.

My sister, like so many other caregivers who shared their stories, also emphasized the importance of using a three-ring notebook to keep track of the tons of medical and insurance information that inevitably come your way when caring for someone with a serious illness. Here's how Sherry described her own notebook.

SHERRY'S STORY

I have learned that keeping a three-ring binder for note taking and gathering my questions for various providers and keeping a history of test results over time has been immeasurably helpful. Doctors laugh at me, but my husband has a surgeon, an oncologist, a primary doctor, social workers, palliative care, physical and occupational therapy—so it all can get very complicated and confusing. I have a separate tab for information about medical insurance and disability issues, one for questions that come up so I can bring them to doctor appointments or have them available for the next hospital visit. I have a tab for lab test results, one for miscellaneous information that I use to jot down equipment we need and who or what transitional care facility lent it to us (walkers, canes, etc.), and I have a thank-you section to keep track of the people who have given or done things for us so I can properly thank them when I have time.

I also have a separate section where I started jotting down things that have brought my husband pleasure or joy. I note names of songs he identifies as "favorites" when he hears them. I jot his answers to questions I ask him about his favorite things in his life now, and I write down poems or thoughts I come across that have special meaning to me or that I might want to share at his memorial service. I jot down people I need to remember to notify, things I need to take care of like investments, life insurance, cell phone plans, possible venues for a gathering, song lyrics that have messages that touch me—all the things that keep me awake in the middle of the night and distract me during the day. They're all in one place so I can refer back and use it as a resource at any time.

I am so grateful to Sherry and the other caregivers who, in the midst of their busy caregiving lives, found the time and had the desire to share all these helpful tips with all of you. These are tried-and-true real-life suggestions from real-life caregivers who discovered through trial and error how to make caregiving responsibilities a bit more manageable, and more than one of them told me that their efforts seemed even more worthwhile if sharing what worked for them helped ease someone else's caregiving burden. Sherry's tips didn't end with the flash drive idea. I found her to be a veritable fountain of caregiver wisdom.

ADDITIONAL TIPS FROM SHERRY

In addition to maintaining my notebook, I also scanned in a lot of information and put it on a flash drive in my purse. It includes my husband's living will, Provider Order of Life Sustaining Treatment, his meds list and doses, a copy of his driver's license, and a copy of the front and back of his medical insurance card. I included disability insurance claim numbers, a list of all his doctors, and their contact information. I also keep hard copies with me. I keep a list of all his meds by his pill organizer as well in case someone else would need to help him fill it, and I gave copies of his living will to our kids and shared the DNR designation information with our children, siblings, and good friends who might happen to be alone with him.

I also created sub-folders in my email for correspondence from his employer, disability insurance provider, and Social Security Administration. I made certain I have the password file for his accounts and user names and passwords for Internet access for anything I may need, including log-ins to his health care providers' patient portals. I made sure all assets and life insurance beneficiaries are properly designated.

It's also a good idea to get a handicapped parking tag as soon as the care receiver has any difficulty with mobility or strength because it makes transporting them to the doctors, etc., so much easier.

And remember—medical services are not always billed correctly, so you should be prepared to do many follow-up calls to a provider and the medical insurance company to get things paid for appropriately. Whenever you have to call anyone for any reason, get their name, and keep a list of all contact people. And remember, you usually get better and faster service if you can keep things friendly.

If there is a trusted friend or family member who is comfortable helping with any of these organizing tasks, Sherry suggested you enlist their help early on because the amount of information that must be collected and organized can be mammoth. Here's what Teresa said.

TERESA'S STORY

I was a happy only child who never missed having siblings, but when my mother was diagnosed with Alzheimer's, I think I would have loved having an accountant brother who could handle all the financial stuff and mounds of other paperwork that comes with caregiving. But I also found certain liberation in being the only go-to person because I could make decisions on Mom's behalf without the hassle of having to clear it with siblings first. She lived in New York, and I live in the Midwest, which made it even tougher. Things got more manageable when I was able to move her here. My husband, kids, and friends have been a big help. It's important for caregivers to have a support system of their own!

Expanding the Circle of Care

When our grandsons were little, they used to love watching the animated children's television show called *Wonder Pets!* in which Linny the Guinea Pig, Tuck Turtle, Ming-Ming Duckling, and other animals work together to solve problems and rescue friends in trouble, all the while singing much of their dialog in somewhat operatic voices. In one of their recurring songs they sing, "What's gonna work? TEAM-work!" We still sing that phrase after all these years when we're doing something together.

I personally think "Teamwork" should be the caregiver theme song, because what has become crystal clear in writing this book is the importance of a solid support system for both the care receiver *and* the primary caregivers. I've seen TEAM used as an acronym to mean Together Each Achieves More, which is so true when it comes to caregiving.

When April, whom we met earlier in this chapter, realized that Craig needed more help than she was able to provide, she wisely formed "Team Craig" and called together friends from all parts of his life—his long-standing volleyball team, his friends from the neighborhood where he was a longtime resident, fellow veterans, friends from his days of working at a community co-op—for an organizational brainstorming meeting. She also asked some of her closest friends to attend as well. She made a big pot of soup, and on a cold winter evening over twenty-five caring souls gathered in her living room to figure out what each could do to support both Craig and April. Since not everyone knew each other, she had put together a photo collage that showed Craig through the decades posing with many of the people in the room. It was a great icebreaker that put everyone at ease.

After recapping the tragic sequence of events and Craig's current status, April invited those present to share their own observations and assessment of his needs. "He gets frustrated 'finding' his words." "He has unsteadiness and weakness walking." "He seems emotionally fragile and confused." "He struggles with short-term memory." "He has difficulty understanding conversations about medications and treatment."

It was unanimously agreed that, given their relationship and her taxing full-time job, April could not be expected to handle the myriad issues surrounding Craig's care on her own, so an executive committee was formed, and people volunteered to take on some of the anticipated tasks, which included

- investigating housing options
- seeing about a power of attorney and health care directive
- investigating medical and county assistance
- having a fundraiser to help with necessary costs
- setting up a visiting schedule and having a visitor's log in Craig's room
- identifying what activities Craig might enjoy and is capable of doing
- setting up a CaringBridge site

Although April still got frequent calls from Craig and various agencies, she said she experienced a surge of relief the night Team Craig came to be.

APRIL'S STORY CONTINUES

I think there's an underlying fear that's hard to express when you feel like you are being depended upon too much. After Craig had his stroke, it got harder for me to do my job. Because of his short-term memory problems, he didn't realize how often he called me, plus I was dealing with his bank, his insurance company, his doctors . . . I started putting all these things on the calendar I keep for my own appointments and clients and was startled by how full it was. No wonder I was tired all the time! Seeing that in black and white motivated me to call on others for help, but that was hard to do because I think we all think we have super powers. This experience reminded me how important it is to ask for and accept help.

Care teams work really well in conjunction with the circle of care and the lists discussed in chapter 4. Although your care team might not be as structured as April's was, complete with an executive committee and check-in meetings, I think it is good to have some structure so members of the caring community aren't duplicating tasks or overwhelming the care receiver or primary caregivers with phone calls or visits. Having a clear idea of what needs to be done and who is most equipped to do whatever job is required saves everyone time and energy. I also suggest naming your team, as April did with Team Craig, because it is an easy and automatic way to communicate more efficiently. When a team member gets an email with Team Craig (or Team Joe or Team Jane, etc.), they automatically know there is news about the care receiver or a favor that requires some attention.

I experienced the importance of teams and communities when close friends who lived on a small farm a few hours away had a horrible house fire. We called together the old gang and had a camp-in on their property. The carpenters and handymen in the group divided their tasks, the gardeners worked outside, others ran errands as needed, cooked, shopped, and watched children. It was like the old times we shared before our lives got busy and complex. We worked together, laughed together, shared food and stories, and after a hard day's work, out came the guitars and we relaxed around a bonfire.

Being a member of a care team is an excellent way for those of us who have a tendency to care*take* and control to exercise our care-*giving* skills because such teams promote a certain interdependency and spirit of cooperation that is harder to experience with "one to one" caregiving. Such participation can give us a way to appreciate, foster, and celebrate community while lessening our need to be the "special one."

Taking Care of the Caregiver

So many of the stories shared in this book underscore the importance of helping the primary caregiver(s) as well as the care receiver. As mentioned in the last chapter, caregiving can take an enormous physical and emotional toll, so sometimes our job as "outer ring" caregivers in the circle of care is to support those closest to the person at the center of care.

In addition to creating a care team, or doing some of the tasks already discussed throughout these pages, here are some other things you may want to consider if you are at a loss of ways to help an often overburdened caregiver:

- Offer to coordinate meal delivery. Internet sites like Meal Train (www.mealtrain.com) are easy to set up and maintain and provide calendars and ways for the care receiver and primary caregiver to communicate dietary needs or schedules. When I've done this, I've put a cooler and container for nonrefrigerated items outside the family's front door with instructions to participants to place their items in these instead of knocking or ringing the bell so as not to disturb individuals who may be resting. I also remind them to label their containers and tape any preparation instructions on them.

- Offer to help set up and maintain an Internet site like Caring-Bridge (www.caringbridge.org). This is a great and expedient way to communicate needs or a person's health status to friends and family so overwhelmed caregivers aren't deluged with phone calls and emails. When a best friend became critically ill on an out-of-country vacation, I found that maintaining her site was a way for me to support her and her family when I couldn't be physically at her side.

- Offer to do specific things like grocery shopping, house chores, vehicle maintenance, tutoring or child care, gardening or lawn care, or minor home repairs.

- Many organizations and clubs have volunteers knit or crochet "care shawls" that are delivered to the care receiver and often an exhausted caregiver as well as a reminder that they are embraced by many who care as they go through a challenging time.

- Provide much-needed respite care for the primary caregiver by offering to spend an afternoon, evening—or even the night if you are close with both people. One of my fondest memories when a friend was recovering from a serious surgery was snuggling with her and watching the entire British television series *Great Expectations* while her husband had a much-needed "play date" with a friend of his own.

- Purchase a massage, a pre-paid VISA card, etc., with the instructions to "Do something special just for yourself."

- Offer to come by to play a favorite game with the caregiver like Scrabble or cards, or bring over a movie you know he or she would enjoy and watch it together.

- Walk their dog or offer to pet-sit if they have to be away from their home for any length of time.

- Help decorate their house for a holiday. One woman I know likes to make Christmas "stocking trees" for care receivers and caregivers. She distributes little stockings to those who want to participate, and people tuck in money that they can use for a special treat.

- Donate vacation days to a coworker/caregiver.

- Give the care receiver and caregiver a weekend away if the care receiver is able to go to a hotel, etc.

- Organize what one creative respondent calls a "rellie rally." When a cousin of hers was going through a difficult divorce, she set a date for a casual potluck for relatives to show their love and support. These gatherings have now become a tradition in this family, and recently one was held for her and her husband, who has advanced melanoma.

These are just some of the things I came up with. What other things would you add to the list? What things would you, as an exhausted or stressed caregiver, most appreciate someone doing for you?

When Caregiving Changes Roles in a Relationship

Remember the person I mentioned earlier who said her role as caregiver made her feel "more nurse than wife"? So many caregivers, like Milt, relayed similar experiences.

MILT'S STORY

I'm a divorced dad, and when I suffered several broken bones and other injuries in a work accident, my kids swooped in to protect and comfort and care for me. It was an overwhelming blessing, but at the same time it felt like a heartbreaking role reversal. I was grateful, of course, to feel the deep love of my children, but

*horrified for them to see me so vulnerable. It was a rite of passage
for all of us that I didn't expect to see for another twenty years at
least. They took turns staying with me, and one night I woke up
during the night and hobbled my way to the bathroom. When I
opened the door to go back to bed, there stood my son waiting for
me. He was so worried about me that he was even watching out
for me while I slept. I was so touched but it also made me a little
sad. I'm supposed to be the one taking care of him.*

Milt's story is a very familiar one for adults who find themselves caring for other adults. As Milt described, it can often be
confusing—even embarrassing—when roles change in a relationship. I think this is especially true at those times when children are
called upon to take care of their parents. I still smile when I think of
the conversation I had with Emily, my 101-year-old friend whom I
introduced you to in chapter 2. When I went to visit her just before
she died, she told me earnestly, as if seeking reassurance, "I think
the kids will be okay if I go." It didn't matter that her "kids" were
middle aged with grown children of their own, or that they had
been overseeing their mom's care for years; she wanted to take care
of *them* right up to the end.

"Caregiving can bring with it a certain kind of intimacy that can
change things," a counselor once explained to me. She said that it's
common for caregivers to feel a sort of "parental responsibility" toward the care receiver and, as a result, relationships often shift. Her
words made me think of the heated exchange I had with my husband
when he was recovering from double knee surgery. I confess I was
being a hovering care*taker*, but he was exasperating me by doing
things his surgeon and physical therapist had cautioned him about
doing—especially when he was taking pain medications. "Don't
treat me like a child!" he bellowed, to which I bellowed back, "Then
stop acting like one!" Luckily we saw the humor in this, and were
able to have a calm strategy session in which we each clearly defined
our respective limits, boundaries, and expectations.

As I discovered in the above example, it's easy to slip into a parental role in caregiving situations, treating an adult care receiver as if he or she was a helpless child. This can be a slippery slope, especially when caring for an elderly person who is no longer able to do all the things they were once capable of doing. It's often difficult for compassionate caregivers to efficiently do what needs to be done in a respectful way that doesn't diminish an individual who took pride in doing those tasks themselves.

Caring for Our Parents or Other Older Adults

I think one of the most dramatic relationship balancing acts takes place when adult children become caregivers for their parents or other older adults. It can get complex and confusing when we find ourselves in a situation where someone who took care of us for a good portion of our lives now has to rely on us to help them with so many aspects of their own lives. Yet, because of medical advancements, greater access to health care, and more economic security with programs like Social Security, Medicare, and Medicaid, people are living much longer than they used to, and caregiving for elders is the reality for millions of families throughout this country.

Most of the changes that occur as people age are gradual, and caregivers and care receivers have time to work together to handle them as they arise. But as so many of the stories in this book demonstrate, unforeseen twists and turns of life can often place us in caring situations we didn't anticipate. When that happens, we just do the best we all can—caregivers and care receivers alike—as we try to figure out and adjust to the new positions we may find ourselves in.

As I wrote in my journal many years ago when I found myself in an unexpected caregiver role, "Sometimes intimacy is thrust upon us." This can get a little awkward when we, as adults, end up assisting a parent or other adult with personal things like dressing, bathing, or going to the bathroom. Things like helping them manage their finances, having uncomfortable conversations about medical issues, or expressing our concerns about their ability to drive or live independently can be difficult as well.

Some caregivers (as well as care receivers) are more comfortable having someone other than immediate family members handle more intimate care tasks, which is totally understandable. Others, like Lorna, have discovered that sometimes such care interactions can add a new dimension of closeness to the caregiving/care receiving relationship.

LORNA'S STORY

My husband and I were my father-in-law's primary caregivers for six years, which allowed him to stay in his own home. A lady from our local CARE organization did light housekeeping and laundry and kept him company two hours a day, and Meals on Wheels delivered meals once a week. Otherwise, we visited every day and did the other things like grocery shopping, clothes shopping, and haircuts. I filled his pillbox once a week and made sure he had taken his meds every day, and I took his blood pressure every day and recorded it.

I would regularly massage his arms with lotion, and once a month I would soak and massage his feet and cut his toenails. It was a joy knowing I was making his life better. One time when I was rubbing lotion on his feet and legs, he looked at me and said, "If I was a cat, I would just purr." Being a cat person myself, I took that as a real compliment. Then he went on to say he had never had anyone take care of his toenails. He said he felt so pampered; I never had to ask twice if he was ready for me to soak his feet!

Lorna and her husband established a regular schedule for visiting her father-in-law, and her special foot soaking and massage ritual helped normalize the necessary toenail cutting task—a task that many caregivers and care receivers have described as embarrassing or distasteful. I think that handling these intimate tasks in as casual a way as possible can help keep the relationship more balanced and less "role-reversed," preserving the dignity of both caregiver and care receiver.

I've had the privilege of having close relationships with several elderly people, and just about all of them have described how difficult it is to become dependent on their children and grandchildren. "I don't want to be a burden," is a phrase I've heard many times, and it's one my own sweet mother repeated more than once when she needed help. These same elders have also confessed to getting frustrated and sometimes a bit angry when family or professional caregivers treat or talk to them as if they were children—something I know from experience is too easy to do, especially during "take-charge" caregiving times when stress is high and patience is thin. Though it sometimes felt like it, and I've seen it often described this way, I tried to remember I wasn't really "parenting my parent" when I cared for my parents. I've come to understand how framing a care interaction as a role-reversed parent/child relationship can lead to talking to or treating a care receiver in a condescending manner that may seem demeaning and risks bruising their sense of dignity.

I had the good fortune of having a wise mother to remind me of who was the parent and who was the child. After her stroke, she gave me an article and poem entitled "I'm Still Me" that spoke to the importance of being able to retain one's identity in the midst of a significant life-changing event. She also gave me an article titled "When It's Time to Take Away Your Parent's Car Keys," so I never had to have *that* conversation with her nor one about finances or documents or assisted living facilities. She always approached such things like a detective, with me as a sidekick, and we figured things out together but with her as the ultimate decision-maker. Although she never had to move to one, we had fun touring and sometimes dining at various senior residences, and she paid a deposit on one we both really liked that was near my home "just in case." Her name came up several times on their list, but she'd simply tell them, "I'm not ready yet," and they'd go on to the next person in line. My husband and Mom and I also went to a university extension class called "Who Gets Grandma's Yellow Pie Plate?" and had fun discussions about who should get each treasured item after she died.

By having her affairs in order, my forward-thinking mother made it easier for me when I became one of her primary caregivers. I learned from her how important it is to "take care of business" *before* lightning strikes or a person becomes necessarily dependent and in need of caregiving, and I urge others to follow her example if it is possible. In fact, it's a good idea for all of us adults—younger and older alike—to have our "just in case" files in order as Mom did (I'll say more about this in the next chapter). But when we're beyond busy with making a living, raising a family, and handling all the things a busy life entails, thinking of things like assisted living or care facilities for ourselves are the last things on our mind—which means these responsibilities fall to the next generation.

Admitting a Loved One to a Care Facility

So many of the caregivers I know have found themselves in the often-difficult position of having to rather suddenly find a nursing home or residential care facility for a loved one. Things get even more complicated when the primary caregiver has to arrange things long distance. Here's what happened to Glen and his dad.

GLEN'S STORY

My dad was very stubborn about leaving his house, but it became unsafe for him to stay there alone. For example, on one visit, I smelled gas and realized he hadn't turned the burner off all the way when he was trying to cook his own lunch. The next month, he fell and broke a hip and could not walk without a walker or climb stairs. He was also showing some signs of dementia. I live in another state, and since there was no other family and he had outlived his close friends, the care professionals I consulted thought it would be best if I moved him near my home. We never had a very good relationship, and when some people asked, "Isn't your dad coming to live with you?" I felt like they might just as well have asked, "Aren't you going to bring an elephant to your house and clean up its shit every day?"

Finally, with the help of a social worker in his county, I persuaded him to give moving a try. I tell you, I definitely needed an impartial adult there to help me. Even then, Dad laid on the guilt. When I was packing up his stuff, he just sat with his head drooped to his chest. I asked him what the matter was, and he said, "I was just practicing for the nursing home." Anyway, I got him moved into a place, and it took a while, but he actually seems pretty content and has made some friends there. We're getting along better, but for the sake of my sanity and our relationship, I need to limit my visits to two a week unless there's an emergency.

Glen's story touches on some emotions and experiences that many caregivers have expressed. Many say they feel a mixture of inadequacy and guilt when they move a loved one to a care facility—even when they know they didn't have the space, the medical equipment, or the means to provide the level of personal, medical, and professional care that was called for. Others, like Glen, are keenly aware of their own and the care receiver's limits, and they realize that for the sake of self and relationship, a "toxic-free" neutral place is the only option that makes sense. A care facility is also the only option for many caregivers who still have children at home when they are called upon to care for an elderly parent.

Such decisions are difficult for everyone involved but, as Glen found, fortunately there are many resources and professional services available to those of you who may be facing them. The websites for the U.S. government's Eldercare Locator (www.eldercare.gov /Eldercare.NET/Public/Index.aspx), Medicare (www.medicare.gov /campaigns/caregiver/caregiver-resource-kit.html), and AARP (www.aarp.org/home-family/caregiving) are good places to start to direct you to resources in your state, and I have included other resources in the back of this book.

In addition to these resources, lots of caregivers benefit from the support they receive in a caregivers' group. The majority of the members of my own group are caring for elderly parents, all of whom reside in care facilities. So many, like Jim, have described our monthly meetings as their lifeline.

JIM'S STORY

I think it's about connecting with a "greater good" outside of yourself. There is a sense of collaboration and mutual appreciation as well as support. It's a safe place where you can think out loud without fear of being corrected or feeling like you need to censor yourself. People truly understand what you're going through because they're going through similar things—which makes you feel a whole lot more normal and a whole lot less guilty when you admit out loud there are days you just don't want to be doing this, and everyone nods their heads in agreement or murmurs, "I know. Me neither."

If you cannot find a caregiver group in your area, check the Internet for online support groups. Many are listed by category or problem, such as cancer support groups, Parkinson's support groups, dementia support groups, and support groups for caregivers of elderly parents.

I encourage you to take the stories, suggestions, and tools we have covered in this chapter into the next, as we talk more about those times when caregiving chooses us. We will also discuss issues that often arise among siblings or mutual caregivers in difficult care situations, as well as feelings of anticipatory grief.

CHAPTER 8

When "Lightning" Strikes

The Special Challenge of Brain Disorders and Dealing with Anticipatory Loss

Taking care of someone is difficult, but you take a lot away;
you gain something very important, a kind of humanity.
It's on the job compassion training.
—GEORGE HODGMAN[1]

We continue the discussion of caregiving in unexpected or often-challenging situations launched in the last chapter. As we'll see in this chapter, the shifting of relationship roles that some caregivers described in previous pages is often poignantly apparent in the face of Alzheimer's disease and other dementia, mental illness, addiction, or other conditions that impair a care receiver's cognitive abilities.

We then move to the topic of anticipatory grief—that often-confusing feeling of loss that many caregivers and care receivers experience in serious, sudden, and/or chronic care situations like those described in this and the preceding chapter. We'll also spend a little time talking about the tension and challenges that often erupt among family members (however you wish to define *family*) in stress-filled care situations.

Alzheimer's and Other Forms of Dementia

Although the terms *dementia* and *Alzheimer's* are often used interchangeably, they do have different meanings. While I won't go into these cognitive disorders in depth, I think it helps to have a brief understanding of what they are.

As experts at the National Institute on Aging explain it, "dementia is the loss of cognitive functioning—thinking, remembering, and reasoning—and behavioral abilities to such an extent that it interferes with a person's daily life and activities."[2] Dementia varies in degree, from mild to severe, and there are several types of dementia, with Alzheimer's being one of them. Other types of progressive and irreversible dementia include the following:[3]

- *Vascular dementia* occurs as a result of damage to the vessels that supply blood to the brain and can be caused by a stroke or other blood vessel condition.

- *Lewy body dementia* is one of the more common types of progressive dementia. It consists of abnormal "clumps" of protein called Lewy bodies, which have also been found in people with Alzheimer's and Parkinson's.

- *Frontotemporal dementia* is a group of diseases that involve the frontal and temporal lobes of the brain (areas generally linked to personality, behavior, and language).

- *Mixed dementia* is a combination of Alzheimer's, vascular dementia, and Lewy body dementia. According to the Mayo Clinic, autopsy studies of the brains of people eighty and older showed that many with dementia had this combination.

As the Mayo Clinic points out, other disorders like Huntington's disease, traumatic brain injury, and Parkinson's disease have been linked to dementia. Sometimes infections, immune disorders, metabolic problems (e.g., thyroid, low blood sugar, etc.), reactions to medications, and other conditions can also cause dementia-like symptoms that can be reversed with treatment.[4]

While dementia is classified as a *group of symptoms* that can affect our memory or ability to reason, Alzheimer's is classified as a *progressive disease* that can cause dementia. According to the National Institute on Aging, the risks for Alzheimer's increase as we age, and in most people with the disease, symptoms first appear in their mid-sixties. It is estimated that over five million Americans have this disease.[5]

In Alzheimer's, an abnormal number of proteins form clumps (called amyloid plaques) and tangled fibers. These plaques and fibers then cause once-healthy neurons (the cells that carry messages from the brain to other parts of the body) to stop functioning as they should. Eventually, they lose their connections with other neurons and die. As more neurons die, additional parts of the brain are affected, and the brain tissue shrinks significantly as the disease progresses. There are three stages to Alzheimer's: an early stage with no symptoms, a middle stage with mild cognitive impairment, and a final stage when Alzheimer's dementia occurs. There is currently no cure for Alzheimer's, and symptoms vary from person to person, as does the progression of the disease. In general, it takes years to develop, and it becomes worse over time to the point that the person with Alzheimer's requires total care.

You can see from this very basic description of Alzheimer's and dementia why it is easy to get confused about cognitive disorders. With their overlapping and similar symptoms, it is often difficult to sort out which behaviors are part of the normal aging process, which ones might be temporary, and which ones are more serious or permanent. The takeaway for caregivers (especially primary caregivers) is that it is important to do your homework if you are caring for someone with these conditions so you have a better understanding of their symptoms and their individual care needs. I encourage you to be selective in your sources of information—go to credible government or medical websites or get information from well-known and well-respected organizations like the Alzheimer's Association. I have also included a list of resources in the back of this book to help you. Many of these resources include helpful tips for caregivers as well as guidance on where they can go for support and further information.

Caring for Someone with Memory Problems

Whatever the cause of the cognitive impairment, I have heard so many stories from caregivers about the challenges that often come when caring for someone with memory problems. Here's how Carl described his wife's short-term memory issues.

CARL'S STORY

My wife had brain surgery for an aneurysm that burst ten years ago and left her with short-term memory loss and other cognitive problems. If you didn't know her, you'd probably just think she's a nice, friendly lady. But her personality changed after this happened. She was always personable and funny, but she went from being a successful business executive who was able to handle tons of things at once—including her family and community involvements—to being this pleasant person who has difficulty doing the things she used to automatically. She had to quit her job because she has trouble taking in or processing information, and she can't manage paperwork, let alone people. And she can't do a lot of things we used to do, like playing board games.

She's such a great sport, and, thanks to the practical and professional support we got, we've all adjusted to this new "normal." But her short-term memory loss can still get to me sometimes, because she can't remember what I just said or who called or what she went into a different room to get. Post-it Notes are our best friend! We have a tablet by the phone, so she's gotten used to writing down the time and who called and the message. When I leave the house, I leave a list of things she wanted to do like dishes or laundry or feeding the cat, and most of the time she remembers to check the items off immediately after she's done them. We have a "clean" and "dirty" magnet on the dishwasher that we are all careful about flipping, and we've all learned not to overwhelm her with a lot of information or by talking too fast or having more than one person talk at a time. It can be challenging, but she makes it easy, and—believe me—it helps to have a sense of humor! She'll say things like "At least I never get bored when you want to watch one of your favorite movies for a second or third time, and think how lucky you are that I can't remember our arguments!"

Carl's story captures just some of the frustrations and challenges that often occur when caring for someone with memory problems. It took time, but, with help, his family developed strategies for coping with his wife's changes. But I know from firsthand experience how absolutely frustrating it can be to care for someone with severe short-term memory loss before those strategies are in place. It's easy to get impatient or treat the person like a child when you have to tell them something over and over and over. It's difficult to have to watch them closely in stores or other crowded places lest they wander or become anxious because they can't find you or because they leave a store, forgetting they haven't paid for an item. That's when that In Case of Emergency card or other "in case of" tactics can come in handy!

I also learned from the time I spent with my memory-impaired friend how absolutely critical it is to also support and help the primary caregiver in these types of situations. They are often exhausted and overwhelmed trying to keep it all (and themselves) together as they try to adjust to this new reality while grieving the way things used to be. If you are in a position to help a primary caregiver who is caring for someone with a cognitive disorder, it is useful to locate your position on the circle of care, then review the suggestions in the previous chapters to think of ways you might care for either the care receiver or caregiver. And if you are the primary caregiver, I encourage you to think about your own support system and what people might do to give you a break.

When the cognitive impairment is permanent and nonprogressive, as it is in Carl's wife's case, those involved have a chance to get somewhat used to the new status quo and, over time, can work together to creatively figure out the best, easiest, and least stressful ways to deal with day-to-day life. However, as Eve discovered, with a progressive disease like Alzheimer's, it's often hard for caregivers to know what to expect or when to expect it.

EVE'S STORY

Looking back, I think something was going on with Mom before she was actually diagnosed with Alzheimer's, but we lived one thousand miles apart, and my dad was good at "covering" for her, so I didn't see it at first. After Dad died, I visited Mom often, and the odd behaviors I noticed seemed to be more than grief reactions. She couldn't figure out money, and she didn't seem to have a good sense of time or place. Things got worse over the next couple of years, and the verdict was Alzheimer's. She became so unpredictable. It was a horrible stage, and our already-rocky relationship got worse. I felt like screaming, "I just want some time off from Alzheimer's!" She had always been my role model for independence, and it broke my heart when I could no longer deal with her as an adult. I was so thankful to get help and support from a wonderful social service agency where she lived, to have them explain, "You have your mother in a different way now." It no longer felt like "me against her," and we worked together to move her to the city where I live.

I got her settled in a memory care place, but she climbed out the window and escaped soon after she arrived. She made it nearly a mile before the police found her. She loved the second place we then moved her to, and things got better. As the disease progressed, she went from being "toxic" to sweet, and we both enjoyed taking Sunday walks and just hanging out—even if she often didn't know who I was. A wonderful therapist helped me select and negotiate boundaries so I could care for Mom with grace instead of resentment. For my own health and sanity (and the sake of my family), I had to set limits by visiting her just once a week plus the care conferences. She couldn't remember if I had been there or not, so I got a journal to write down when I had visited. It was a great tool—a visual aid that also allowed the nursing staff to reassure her I had been there. They were terrific and never made me feel guilty for not visiting more. And I don't know what I'd do without my caregivers' group—supportive people who truly know the difference between feeling "carefree" and "careworn." My experience has cracked open my compassion for others even more.

As is poignantly clear from Carl's and Eve's stories, everyone's world seems to shift when Alzheimer's or other memory loss and cognitive problems invade it. Caregivers—both primary and secondary—often struggle with how to best navigate this new way of being with the least amount of frustration and the greatest amount of respect. I think of it as being lost in the "bewilderness."

As I mentioned, thanks to the Internet and organizations like the Alzheimer's Association and Family Caregiver Alliance, if they have access to a computer, caregivers can find immediate guidance and more suggestions than I am able to include here at their fingertips. It's always important, though, to use reliable sources and double-check information if questions arise or something is unclear.

Because there are so many types of cognitive disorders, and because these problems can manifest differently from individual to individual, it is important that each caregiver do their own digging to get the specific information *and* the appropriate support for their individual needs. However, I've compiled some general suggestions for relating to a person with Alzheimer's or dementia that you may find useful in the meantime.

- It helps to have eye contact, identify yourself, and say their name when beginning a conversation ("Hi Jake; it's Joe"), and speak slowly in a calm, gentle way that doesn't relate frustration or excitement because people with dementia often mirror what they see or sense.

- Straightforward, simple sentences are usually best, and because it can embarrass the person if they don't know an answer, it's usually best to avoid questions or ask only those that require a yes or no answer. Remember to give the person time to process information or instructions. ("Let's put our coats on.")

- Try to be patient and supportive; avoid correcting, arguing, or quizzing; and keep your expectations in check about what they can do or remember. It helps to tune in to their tone of voice, actions, and feelings to understand what they are trying to communicate because they often may say one word but mean another.

- People with memory loss often forget important things, like the death of a loved one, so reminding them of the loss can be painful or confusing. Instead of saying, "Your wife died, Jake," experts suggest asking them to tell you something about the person they mentioned.

- The world can seem confusing, frightening, and frustrating for those with Alzheimer's and other dementia, so try to be reassuring and understanding. It is common for them to lose track of time, so they may feel deserted if you leave for even a few minutes because it feels much longer to them.

- Try to "go with the flow." People with Alzheimer's sometimes lose a sense of reality. It can just lead to frustration for both of you if, for example, you try to convince them you are their daughter, not their college roommate or new friend.

- Using song lyrics or familiar verses can help with communication, and when conversation is difficult, it is often reassuring to listen to music or hold their hand or gently massage their arm.

- Help the person get adequate exercise, as Eve did when she and her mother would take regular walks. Many care facilities have regular activities, so it's a good idea to find out which the person may enjoy, but try to be flexible because they may have a short attention span.

- Using a visual aid like a photograph or magazine picture can be helpful. Writing things down is also a good idea, as Eve did when she recorded her visits in a journal.
- Persons with memory problems may not be able to judge what is safe or unsafe, so take precautions to avoid potentially dangerous situations.

Caring for people with cognitive problems can be extremely taxing, *so remember to take care of yourself!* Try to find appropriate support services, consider joining a support group, review the self-care suggestions in this book, and don't be afraid to ask for what *you* need. Let others care for you as you care for your loved one.

In addition to the tips I found, Gwen shared some of the things she did for her mother.

GWEN'S STORY

When Mom was first moved to a memory care facility, I stored some of her favorite games in her closet, and we'd play them when I visited. She loved for me to do her nails and massage her hands, and for me to go with her to activities there. I really believe that kept her more alert. As the Alzheimer's progressed, she eventually forgot how to walk or eat, so I tried to get there for one meal a day to help her because she seemed to eat better if I did that. I made two photo albums for her to help keep her connected to the family—pictures from her dating years with Dad, some of her siblings, and some of us kids. The second album contained pictures of her grandchildren and great-grandchildren. She loved babies, so on the blank pages at the end, I placed pictures of babies cut out from magazines. She loved looking at those books! There are so many losses with Alzheimer's, but there are beautiful things

too—each of those moments was like a brand new experience
with so much joy in simple things. I also found a blanket with a
picture of two beautiful little children with wings. When I brought
it to her, she grabbed it and said, "Come to Grandma," as though
they were real children. She loved that blanket, and it covered her
legs in the casket when she died.

As difficult as caring for someone with cognitive problems can
be, Gwen's story of sweet moments was similar to experiences many
caregivers in similar situations related to me. They talked of singing
old songs together, taking walks or long car rides, and shared tender
stories of learning to just be in and appreciate special moments.
One man I know had a wife who'd had frontotemporal dementia for
years. He visited her every day, even after she couldn't communicate
with or recognize him. When I said how sorry I was, he immediately
said, "Oh, don't feel sorry; it's a privilege to care for her, and we
promised 'till death.' I love to bring my guitar and sing for her and
the other residents. They enjoy it so much, and so do I."

Of course, I've also heard heartbreaking stories of loved ones
whose personalities changed or of otherwise gentle people who
became violent because of a disease like Alzheimer's. And many
caregivers—completely worn out from years of caring for someone
they lost "a little at a time"—admitted how sad, yet relieved, they
were when their loved one finally died. I have heard this expressed
in the presence of other caregivers in similar situations, all of whom
were quick to reassure them with words like "I know. Me too. Try
not to feel guilty." If you are one of the careworn caregivers that Eve
described, I hope you hear their words and embrace their message,
knowing you do not walk this path alone.

Even in the midst of such pain, loss, exhaustion, and confusion,
many also stressed the importance of keeping a sense of humor.
Pam, a friend of mine whose mom was diagnosed with Alzheimer's
ten years ago, shared the following memory.

PAM'S STORY

Mom was in a memory care facility but still willing and able to have us take her out for special occasions. At that time, she could still eat by herself, use the bathroom alone, and admire things without moving or hiding or rearranging them. She could still admire green lawns or lakes. After one Easter family dinner at my house, Mom thanked me for the nice meal, commented on our nice family, then said, "Do you know what I wish?" "What Mom?" my sister and brother and I all asked. "At times like this, I really wish I had children." We are still able to laugh about that memory; sometimes with Alzheimer's, that's all you can do. Then you go off to another corner of grief and look for the cracks of light—she still responds to hands that hold and hugs that enfold. She still likes to sit outside and look at the flowers in the planters outside the facility. So, here we are. But we are so ready.

Caring for Someone with Mental Illness

According to the National Alliance on Mental Illness (NAMI), "A mental illness is a condition that affects a person's thinking, feeling, or mood."[6] As NAMI explains, each person with a mental illness has different experiences—even the people with the same diagnosis. According to them, one in five adults experiences a mental health condition every year, and one in seventeen lives with a serious mental illness like schizophrenia or bipolar disorder. Some illnesses are temporary, some long lasting. Some occur in childhood and some later in life, but the effects of mental illness can be far-reaching— from the family to work or school to the community and beyond—and the caregiving needs are great for both the person with the illness and their primary caregivers. Unlike Alzheimer's, which is progressive, mental illness can be cyclical, with possible ups and downs and stable "in-betweens."

NAMI states that "mental health professionals have effective treatments for most of these conditions, yet in any given year, only

60 percent of people with a mental illness get mental health care. As a result, family members and caregivers often play a large role in helping and supporting them."[7] Some of those without treatment don't have access to it; others may be unwilling to get it. When it goes untreated—and even when it is under control with medications and appropriate therapy—families dealing with mental illness often live in their own state of "bewilderness" as they worry and fear for their loved one. Parents strive to get help for their child with attention-deficit/hyperactivity disorder (ADHD) or autism; families worry about vulnerable loved ones with bipolar or borderline disorder or depression, PTSD, or the number of other mental disorders that strike people each and every day. Are they safe? Are they suicidal? Do they need help? Can we get them the help they need? Are they taking their meds? Can we trust that this calm will last?

In a recent public radio program, a NAMI representative called mental illnesses one of the "no hot dish" illnesses—it's not one of those conditions where neighbors usually drop off food, offer help and support, or send get-well cards. Often, people who might help may not be aware there is a need for support. Or perhaps the stigma that often accompanies mental illness prevents them from doing so because, as James discovered, people don't understand that it is a "no-fault," brain-based illness that can be managed and treated.

JAMES'S STORY

When our teenage daughter kept losing weight, we were worried, and many who knew our family were concerned about all of us. We all thought it was a disease like cancer. Close friends checked in, sent cards, and said they were praying for us. When she was diagnosed with a serious eating disorder, then was hospitalized, I think people didn't know what to do, and most of the support disappeared. My wife and I both took off work so we could go to family meetings and other appointments. One coworker I thought was a friend actually made a snide comment about me missing work because my daughter was "just acting out." Here we were, feeling scared and powerless, and he was being heartless.

As James's story illustrates, caregivers often feel helpless, overwhelmed, isolated, and abandoned when there is mental illness in a family. This is why it is important for them to connect with organizations like NAMI, good friends, or other support systems. Overwhelmed primary caregivers often need a "mental health" day for themselves when their loved one is in crisis. And caregivers who are called upon to take care of schedules, bills, day care, transportation, medications, and the many other needs for an adult or child with a severe mental disability—including those with intellectual disabilities such as fetal alcohol syndrome and Down syndrome—often benefit from having a care team in place they can activate when the need arises. If I had a magic wand, I would refund all the agencies and social services and insurance benefits that have disappeared over the years so families with mental illnesses could get the help they so desperately need. Until then, it's up to compassionate caregivers to fill those voids. If you know of someone in this situation, I urge you to ask yourself, "How might I help?" Even a small gesture of kindness can go a long way.

Alcoholism and Other Drug Addictions

I can't end the discussion of challenging care situations covered in these two chapters without mentioning alcohol and drugs. Many adults with mental illness abuse alcohol or other drugs in an attempt to medicate or numb their mental pain, and this abuse can lead to addiction. And sometimes a substance use disorder like alcohol or drug addiction can even cause a mental disorder. When people have both a mental disorder and a substance use disorder, they are said to have co-occurring or dual disorders. Fortunately, co-occurring disorders can be effectively treated at the same time. Because antidepressants and other necessary medications for mental health disorders are not considered addictive, professionals—as well as many recovery groups like Alcoholics Anonymous (AA) and Narcotics Anonymous (NA)—accept that those with co-occurring disorders can take them and still be considered "clean and sober."[8]

But alcohol or other drug abuse can be a problem for *both care receivers and caregivers* in any of the situations described in this and the previous chapter. We are a society that longs for quick fixes, and when a crisis occurs or we feel overwhelmed by the stress and demands that serious illnesses and diseases bring with them, it is tempting and so very understandable to want to have a drink, smoke a joint or cigarette, or pop a pill in an attempt to relax or numb the pain. While most people can drink or even use certain drugs on occasion and stop when they want to with no obvious problems, others seem unable to control their drinking or other drug use, no matter how hard they try on their own.

This can be especially challenging to deal with when someone becomes addicted to prescription painkillers like OxyContin, Vicodin, fentanyl, or codeine. Addiction to and overdoses with these drugs have become an epidemic, with users often turning to the cheaper, stronger heroin readily available on the streets when their pills are cut off. Caregivers need to pay special attention to those who are using opioid painkillers for short-term or chronic pain, to monitor their use and talk to their medical providers for safer alternatives for pain relief if use turns to abuse.

If you worry about your own use of alcohol or other drugs, many websites like that of the National Council on Alcoholism and Drug Dependence (NCADD) or AA offer self-tests for those who suspect they have a problem. As NCADD cautions, however, these tests are only meant to inform—not diagnose. It is important that you consult a qualified professional for a full evaluation if you think you might have a substance abuse problem.

And if you are a caregiver who is already in an addiction recovery group, remember that caregiving can be stressful and exhausting, which can make you more vulnerable to relapse. An important part of self-care is making certain you carve out the time you need to go to meetings, keep up your regular meditation or other recovery practices, get adequate sleep, and connect with your sponsor or a group friend if and when you need to.

Caring and Codependency

As many of the caregivers in this book have described, sometimes a loved one's substance use disorder is *the* problem in a household, all on its own. An alcohol or other drug disorder is a diagnosable brain disease that can be managed but not cured—which is why people who stop drinking or using drugs are said to be "in recovery," rather than "recovered." Although addicts are not responsible for their disease, they are responsible for managing it—just as diabetics are responsible for managing their disease. Addictions are called family diseases for a reason. Here's how the book *Recovery Now* explains it:

> Regardless of circumstances, addiction is called a family disease because one member's addiction affects the whole family— whether or not its members are related by blood or by some other bond. When we actively practice addiction, our family members usually adjust by taking on certain survival roles. A non-addicted spouse or parent might take over running the household, becoming the family decision maker, or do things to cover up or try to make up for our addictive behavior. An older child might become the "responsible one," trying to take care of things when an addicted parent is unable to do so. One child might try to make things better by attempting to be perfect and another by becoming "invisible." Someone else in the family might act the clown, or just act out to get attention or draw attention away from the real problem—addiction.[9]

Think for a moment of how I defined *codependency* in the introduction to this book. I described codependency as the *out-of-balance behavior of someone who is overinvolved* in another person's life. Now reread the above definition through the lens of codependent care*taking*. What behaviors or words jump out at you? How about "take over running the household," being the "decision maker," doing "things to cover up" someone's addictive behavior, becoming the "responsible one," or acting out "to get attention"?

If someone in your family is struggling with alcoholism or other drug addiction, and you find yourself adopting codependent care*taking* behaviors, I urge you to get appropriate support and help for yourself and your children. Regardless of whether your loved one is acting responsibly, you can practice good self-care and not get sucked into the pit of family dysfunction that addiction can create. Twelve Step groups like Al-Anon, Alateen, Nar-Anon, or Co-Dependents Anonymous are good places to start, and their contact information can be found in the resource section. Participants do not offer advice; they share their stories and offer mutual support. Among other things, an appropriate support group or a qualified therapist can help caregivers establish healthy balance and boundaries by learning to practice "detaching with love." This self-care technique doesn't mean threatening to leave if an addict doesn't stop drinking or using drugs; it is about letting go of our need and attempts to control their behavior. It is about sending the no-strings-attached message "I care about you enough to let you take responsibility for your own life, just as I take responsibility for mine."

Anticipatory and Ambiguous Grief

No matter where they find themselves in the circle of care, caregivers in serious or challenging care situations like the ones described in this and the previous chapter, and in stories throughout the book, may struggle with what I call "anticipatory grief"—although I'm sure I didn't invent that term. I think of anticipatory grief as the sadness and impending grief we often feel when a loved one gets a serious or terminal diagnosis that changes future plans; when a family faces the uncertainty that mental illness or brain disorders can bring; or when mixed feelings erupt before a divorce, an operation, or an upcoming job layoff.

Caregivers who care for a loved one with Alzheimer's and other dementia often describe an uneven path of grief that begins at diagnosis and ebbs and flows as the disease progresses. Caregivers who worry about children who are in gangs, who are engaging in risky or suicidal behavior, or who are entering military service often describe similar feelings.

Caregivers and care receivers who experience anticipatory grief may have feelings of dread, anxiety, helplessness, hopelessness, guilt, confusion, despair, or even anger. As my forty-five-year-old cousin Chris described it when she got a terminal cancer diagnosis, "I'm mad at my husband because he gets to live and experience marriages and grandchildren. He's angry with me because I'm going to die and leave him and the boys."

I still recall the overwhelming feelings of loss I had when my husband was diagnosed with PTSD. I remember feeling I had no right to grieve because he was still alive and our little family was intact. My therapist called this feeling "ambiguous loss" and helped me understand how important it is to acknowledge the grief we feel when lives and relationships change. She made me see how normal, even common, my feelings were and how having them didn't mean we wouldn't grow stronger as a result of the experience—which we did. Being given this "permission" to grieve was a precious gift that helped me cope with, then emerge from, the intermittent depression I tried to ignore for such a long time.

In my book *Shock Waves*, where I described that experience, I called grief "a messy process." Despite the talk of grief happening in stages, I think of the grief process as more of a nonlinear experience—a feeling like we're trying to swim through mud. I came to understand that grief—whether anticipatory or the "actual" grief we experience when someone dies—can be cumulative if we try to ignore it.

C. S. Lewis wrote, "No one ever told me that grief felt so like fear." This makes sense to me—especially when thinking about the complexity of caregiving in serious circumstances. Here's how Jane described this.

My husband had a stroke that affected him both mentally and physically. Having a cognitively impaired partner is very lonely and puts a tremendous amount of pressure on me. I have to take care of everything—pay all the bills, arrange all his therapies, organize his social life, handle paperwork, interpret the world for him, make all phone calls, set up what little work he can do, be his memory and also his home-based exercise and therapy coach. We used to function as a single organism, and I think the hardest thing now is knowing that my husband will not be able to care for me if I become infirm. He is unable to pick up on emotional cues and unable to see if I am unwell unless I tell him. The best help I've received was from close friends who allowed me to talk about my fears and sadness.

If you, like Jane, are a caregiver who is experiencing the feelings described in this section, know that these are normal reactions to the uncertainty that often accompanies some of the situations I've described. As I discovered, it helps to acknowledge those feelings and seek support from a trusted friend, a therapist, or a support group. Working through these complicated feelings doesn't mean they'll go away, but we can learn to carry them in a way that makes more room for compassionate caregiving.

Having the "Conversation" *before* Lightning Strikes

Perhaps this is a good time to mention The Conversation Project, which began in 2010 when journalist Ellen Goodman and a group of colleagues and concerned media, clergy, and medical professionals gathered to talk about how they wanted to live at the end of their lives. From those talks came the idea for a grassroots campaign with the goal of making it easier for people everywhere to initiate conversations about dying *now* and as often as necessary so their wishes are known when the time comes.[10]

According to the Conversation Project website (www .theconversationproject.org), its 2013 national survey, and the 2012 California HealthCare Foundation survey it cites,

- 90 percent of Americans say that talking to their loved ones about end-of-life care is important, but only 27 percent have actually done so.

- 80 percent of people say that if seriously ill, they would want to talk to their doctor about wishes for medical treatment toward the end of life, but only 7 percent report having had these conversations.

- 60 percent of people say that making sure their family is not burdened by tough decisions is extremely important, yet 56 percent have not communicated their end-of-life wishes.

- 82 percent of people say it's important to put their wishes in writing, yet only 23 percent have actually done it.

The conversation isn't just about filling out advance directives or other medical or legal forms; it's about talking with loved ones about end-of-life choices. As Ellen Goodman says, it's about values—"what matters to you, not what's the matter with you."

As the stories in this book reveal, "lightning" can strike at any time, so it's important for everyone—from young adults to the elderly—to be talking about these important issues now. The Conversation Project makes it easy. It provides a free kit and guide for having these important conversations with each other and with doctors, and a special kit for those who are dealing with Alzheimer's and dementia. Resources are also available for families caring for loved ones with cognitive disorders to help these caregivers navigate end-of-life discussions based on the cognitive level of the impaired. Kits are available in French, Hebrew, Korean, Mandarin, Russian, Spanish, and Vietnamese.

The idea of having these conversations is catching on, and The Conversation Project has a community resource center for organizations that want to launch these conversations. For example, a church in St. Paul hosted months of facilitated small-group discussions with the goal of having 100 percent of all families in the church completing end-of-life documents that speak to their individual end-of-life wishes.

Get Out of "Jail" Free

I want to close these two chapters and discussion of caregiving in difficult situations by addressing the conflict that can arise when emotion is deep and tension is high. Friction often occurs in families, especially among siblings. As the Family Caregiver Alliance states,

> Invariably, the demands of caregiving bring out old patterns and unresolved tensions. Past wounds are reopened and childhood rivalries reemerge. It is not unusual for adult children to find themselves replaying their historical roles in the family, recreating old dynamics of competition and resentment. . . .[11]

Family dynamics is an often-discussed topic in my caregivers' group, as members talk about the various caregiving challenges they deal with in their families: the arguments about care decisions, the hard feelings that arise when one sibling feels they are doing more than another, trust issues about finances and inheritances, and strong opinions about end-of-life care or memorial services. Resentments surface. Exhaustion and grief get in the way of closeness and love. I can attest to how easily this can occur.

My older sister and I are best friends. Although we don't live near each other, we talk on the phone almost every day. We vacation together and love each other unconditionally, and we loved our parents fiercely and worked together to care for them in their final days. Yet even then, when our emotions were raw and we were beyond tired from all there was to do, we would revert back to being ten and twelve years old. One time, I even locked myself in the bathroom and, when I heard her approach, I began screaming, "Just leave me the hell alone!"

When I facilitate our caregivers' group, I frequently hand out two wallet-size cards. One has a quote by Mary Anne Radmacher: "Courage doesn't always roar. Sometimes courage is the little voice at the end of the day that says I'll try again tomorrow."

I also give them many copies of a Get Out of "Jail" Free card, suggesting they distribute a few to each of their fellow family caregivers so whoever needs to can "play" theirs by way of apology when they've done or said something that created unnecessary friction. I confess that I actually gave one to my sister after that embarrassing scene described above! And we've used several since then as a way to defuse tense moments. I've included a page of Get Out of "Jail" Free cards in appendix F that I invite you to copy and use in similar situations.

Here are some other suggestions from the Family Caregiver Alliance for resolving conflict or defusing tension that other families may want to consider:[12]

- Express your feelings honestly and directly. Let your siblings know their help is both wanted and needed.

- Keep family members informed regarding a parent's condition.

- Be realistic in your expectations. Allow siblings to help in ways they are able and divide tasks according to individual abilities, current life pressures, and personal freedoms. Assistance with errands, finances, legal work, or other indirect care may be the best option for some family members.

- Express appreciation to your family for the help they are able to provide.

- Accept siblings for who they are and expect differences of opinion.

- Try to respect others' perceptions and find opportunities to compromise.

- If communication is particularly contentious, arrange a family meeting that includes an outside facilitator, such as your Family Caregiver Alliance Family Consultant, social worker, counselor, religious leader, or friend. A trusted outside party can ensure that everyone's voice is heard.

- If siblings are unable to help with care, seek other assistance to provide a respite for yourself. Call your local Caregiver Resource Center, Area Agency on Aging, senior center, or other community resource to locate help.

Caregiving is a balancing act, and family members are like a pyramid of acrobats. Try to do your best not to tumble and bruise. Try to be as gentle and forgiving with each other and with yourself as you can be. And if all these suggestions fail, play that Get Out of "Jail" Free card, pick yourself up, and, if you can, don't forget to laugh. In the next chapter, we'll look toward the future by discussing the concept of "paying it forward" by nurturing future generations of compassionate caregivers and the importance of service to others.

CHAPTER 9

Raising Compassionate Children and Paying It Forward

It's not our job to toughen our children up to face a cruel and heartless world. It's our job to raise children who will make the world a little less cruel and heartless.

—L. R. KNOST, *TWO THOUSAND KISSES A DAY: GENTLE PARENTING THROUGH THE AGES AND STAGES*[1]

In the last two chapters, we talked about those times when caregiving "chooses" us, and how we can best take care of ourselves or help primary caregivers in serious and unexpected situations. This final chapter talks about the importance of nurturing compassion in children and the concepts of paying it forward and caring as service. Then we'll wrap things up with some final tips and suggestions.

Children and Kindness

During a recent sleepover, our ten-year-old twin grandsons asked me about the new book I was writing. I told them it was about caregiving, and that I was working on a chapter about children and kindness. "Where do you think kids learn to be kind?" I asked them. "From their parents and environment," they agreed, going on to talk about how their school teaches them not to be bullies, and how they have special events where they make up sandwiches and raise money for a homeless shelter for families.

Although they did not mention it at the time, I also thought of the "Rules of the Household" their parents hung on the wall when they were just toddlers. It reads, "Listen the first time. Use your hands and words respectfully. Clean up when it's time." These happy boys are raised in a home where they listen and are listened to with respect and without interruption; where laughter is encouraged and feelings are honored and acknowledged; and where good manners are expected. It is a warm, safe, and peaceful place to be.

"Why do you think it's important to be kind to others?" was my next question. "Because it makes the world a better place. Because people like you better when you're nice," was the response. Then one of them added, by way of an example, "It's important for rich people to give to others and not keep all the money for themselves. So many people who don't have as much as they do need so many things, so they should share some of what they have." I know about the significance of taking advantage of "teachable moments," but in this case, it felt like they were teaching me—not the other way around.

Teachable Moments

Teachable moments are those big and small moments when children seem most ready to learn. They are opportunities to connect to children on a deeper level and a chance to practice and model attentive listening and good communication skills, to let them know who we are and what we value, and to find out more about who they are and what's important to them. As Emma related, teachable moments can also be tools for connection and community building.

EMMA'S STORY

Years ago, after my husband and daughter and I took part in the first Martin Luther King birthday march in our town, I received a vile letter from an anonymous person who had read a small, harmless quote by me in an article about the march. I shook when I opened the envelope filled with white supremacist

hate pamphlets and a handwritten note that called me "a piece
of white vomitous trash" because I had chosen to honor a black
leader.

Several friends and their children happened to be visiting us
at the time I received this hate mail, and we used the experience
as a teachable moment. We sat in a circle in our living room, and
each person had a turn to talk about anger and hate and preju-
dice. After the discussion, we ceremonially burned the packet in
the fireplace, and vowed one by one that we would do our best to
work for peace and justice.

Experts caution that, while we want to give children accurate
information, we should take care not to scare them or give them
more details than are suitable for their age or level of maturity. They
suggest using open-ended questions like "How did that make you
feel?" or "What do you think about that?" And adults should take
care to use "I" statements that address their own feelings and beliefs rather than telling children how they should feel or what they
should believe. They also suggest paying attention to body language.
If you're met with children's blank faces and faraway stares, the lesson would likely be lost on them, so it is probably best to wait for
another teachable moment.

Mixed Messages

Remember the discussion of empathy in chapter 5 that mentioned
how some researchers contend that most of us are born with "seeds"
of empathy already in us? While that may be true, I believe those
seeds must be tended in order to sprout and grow. Each attempt at
connection with children, each time we listen to them respectfully,
and each time we take advantage of teachable moments, as Emma
did in the above story, helps children develop their instincts for
compassionate caring. But, as a recent Harvard study shows, too
often children are getting mixed messages from adults about what
values are most important.

According to researchers at the Harvard Graduate School of Education's Making Caring Common Project, there is a gap between what parents and other adults *say* is most important and the real messages adults convey to children through their actions and reactions. For example, while research shows that most parents and teachers say that developing caring children is more important than their achievements, that's not the message kids are getting from them. In a survey Harvard conducted, they asked ten thousand diverse middle and high school students from thirty-three schools across the nation to rank what was most important to them: achieving at a high level, happiness (feeling good most of the time), or caring for others. Almost 80 percent of the youth ranked achievement or happiness as most important, while only 20 percent chose caring for others.[2]

Guess where they got that message? About 80 percent of the youth surveyed said their parents and teachers would also rank achievement or happiness the highest. These same youth were three times more likely to agree with the statement "My parents are prouder if I get good grades in my classes than if I'm a caring community member in class and school."[3]

But take heart. While the Harvard research reflects a weak commitment to the common good and lack of focus on societal well-being, the researchers also found that caring and fairness still do count—it's just that individual accomplishments appear to outweigh these qualities, so there are reasons to be concerned.

As the Harvard report "The Children We Mean to Raise: The Real Messages Adults Are Sending About Values" emphasizes, when youth think personal success and happiness are more important than caring or fairness, they are at greater risk for many forms of harmful behavior, including cruelty, disrespect, and dishonesty.[4] Plus, when so much attention is given to achievement, there is a higher likelihood for stress and the negatives that the drive for success and perfection can hold. As the report stresses,

The solution is straightforward, but not easy. To begin, we'll have to stop passing the buck. While Americans worry a great deal about children's moral state, no one seems to think that they're part of the problem. As adults we all need to take a hard look at the messages we send to children and youth daily.

Encouraging Compassionate Caring

It is easy to blame peer groups, the educational system, teachers, or the media for an increasing shift in priorities from interest in the common good to self-interest, but as the Harvard project points out, all adults who interact with children share responsibility. They say we should ask ourselves if we're "walking our talk" when we tell our children how important it is to care for those beyond ourselves and our immediate circle.

> It will mean doing a kind of reckoning, a check on our messages about happiness and achievement in contrast to our messages about caring and fairness. Do we regularly tell our children, for example, that "the most important thing is that you're happy," or do we say that "the most important thing is that you act with integrity and are kind"? Do we insist that our children are not rude to us or never treat people offhandedly? Do we insist that our children do the right thing even if it doesn't make them happy or successful? Do we remind our children of their obligations to their communities, for example, their classrooms and schools, their teams and school choirs, and their neighborhoods? Do we place consistent ethical demands on our children not only when it collides with their happiness and achievements but when they may be furious at us, when it threatens our *own* happiness?[5]

These are, in my opinion, critical questions that we, as compassionate caregivers and responsible citizens, should ask ourselves often. As you review the following suggestions I've compiled, consider which of these you might like to try out.

- Model respect and politeness, and make practices like saying, "Thank you for the nice meal" or other expressions of appreciation routine. Try to give children advanced warning instead of abruptly ending an enjoyable activity they may be engaged in. For example, you might say, "It's almost dinnertime, kids. Ten minutes to wrap it up."

- Honor and talk about feelings when appropriate, instead of belittling or dismissing them. How many of us like "just get over it" messages? As experts point out, acknowledging feelings doesn't mean you necessarily agree with their reactions or behavior; it shows children you care about and understand them. After acknowledging feelings, you can work together with children to come up with some solutions to avoid similar problems in the future.

- Practice and encourage active *and* attentive listening and communication, and discourage interrupting when someone is talking. Foster empathy by discussing other viewpoints. The developers of the Harvard program call this "zooming in" and "zooming out"; paying attention to the people present, then considering the bigger picture, including perspectives of people like the unpopular student, the janitor, or the new student who may not speak English.

- Consider letting a child assume some of the responsibility for pet care. It can be a great way for them to practice compassionate caregiving.

- Take advantage of teachable moments. For example, encourage ethical thinking by engaging children in *mutual* conversation when a problem or dilemma is presented in a television show or in a movie. We like to watch episodes of the old family TV show *Leave It to Beaver* with our grandsons, for example, because so many of the issues that the youngest son grapples with mirror our grandsons' experiences.

- Try to limit screen time—your own and a child's—and spend more time doing something creative together. Try an art project. Brainstorm a "treasure hunt" list together of things you might find on a walk in the city or a hike in the woods, and set out together to find the items. Read an age-appropriate book out loud as a family. For instance, good friends of mine talk fondly of reading all the *Harry Potter* books out loud with their son well into his teen years.

- Try playing a cooperative family board game where no one wins unless everyone wins, like Race to the Treasure for younger children and families, Forbidden Island (ten and up), or Pandemic (ten and up).

- Take an active interest in their world. For example, I recall being in a restaurant and overhearing a mom in the next booth ask her two young children what seemed like a great, daily after-school ritual, "What did you learn today, and what made you smile?"

- Use the TEAM approach discussed in chapter 7 and elsewhere in this book to tackle household tasks and projects.

- Encourage empathy by tuning children in to voice inflections and facial expressions. It might be fun to use the Greater Good Science Center's online quiz about reading emotions discussed in chapter 5 as a tool for discussion (see http:// greatergood.berkeley.edu/ei_quiz).

- Express and show genuine affection. In addition to making it okay to say "I love you" within a family, think about doing things like writing individual "just for you" notes or special letters on a holiday or birthday that communicate your pride for who your children are now *and* who they are becoming.

These are some of the things I came up with. What others can you think of? Ideally, compassionate and caring children also learn to be compassionate and caring members of society. As we discussed in chapter 5, helping others not only benefits an individual, it can increase our capacity for empathy, and it's actually good for our emotional and physical health. Here are some things you may want to try with children to encourage their respect, kindness, and compassion in the wider community.

- Model kindness, patience, and gratitude to children by taking time to thank a server at a restaurant, a librarian, a gas attendant, a retail clerk, a school janitor, and others.

- Organize a work team of mixed ages to help seniors in the community with lawn care or other chores.

- Enlist children to go with you to prepare or serve meals at a family homeless shelter or similar place.

- Brainstorm with children about service projects you might want to do together and/or engage them in occasional conversations about caring and uncaring acts they might have witnessed or heard. (Try to listen, not lecture.)

- Encourage children to talk about acts of justice or injustice they might witness or hear about (e.g., a fellow student who stands up for a person being bullied, or a person in the community or in the news who is working to combat prejudice).

- Look for opportunities to introduce children to diverse groups of children and adults—perhaps those of different cultures, races, ages, or economic status, or those with physical or mental challenges.

- Encourage children to donate some of their toys, books, or clothes to families who have experienced a loss because of a fire or natural disaster.

- Participate in organizations (e.g., scouting, community, athletic, or religious organizations) that respect and support children, that promote cooperation and teamwork, that provide opportunities for community service, and that support adults who care for children. I love the message an adult leader communicated to children at a recent end-of-summer family gathering at our church. He acknowledged how normal it is to feel a bit nervous before school starts. Then he gave each child a container of stars for their backpack, telling them, "Each star represents a person in this community. So if you are feeling scared or lonesome, look at all those stars and know that you travel with the love and support of all of us."

- Encourage children to engage in random acts of kindness (e.g., having lunch with a student who is new to the class, or shy, or being left out; doing an unexpected favor for a parent or sibling). According to researchers at the University of British Columbia, such acts can have measurable benefits. They did a study with nine- to eleven-year-olds in nineteen classrooms. Some children were asked to perform three acts of kindness (e.g., give Mom a hug when she is stressed, share lunches, vacuum floors), and the others were asked to visit three tourist attractions. After four weeks, they found that all the children had more positive emotions, but the children who performed acts of kindness became more empathetic and accepting of peers, and their behavior made them more popular.[6]

In addition to my list, I encourage you to add your own ideas for promoting respect, kindness, and caring—all ingredients of compassionate caregiving. And how about including children in your own actual caregiving activities? So often, children's imaginations can get the better of them when there is a serious illness or concern in the family and good-intentioned adults seem secretive or distant in efforts to protect them. Caregivers Alison, Rex, and Megan offered the following suggestions for ways to involve children.

ALISON'S STORY

I was so impressed and grateful at the way my adult children handled my husband's terminal cancer diagnosis with their children.

Although they had been told of his illness, four of our grandchildren hadn't seen Papa for months, so their parents prepared them ahead of time. They were told that even though their grandfather looked very different on the outside because of the cancer and treatments, he was still Papa on the inside, although he wouldn't be able to do all the fun activities they used to do. They were encouraged to talk about their feelings, and they brainstormed things they could do to help me, and quiet but fun activities Papa might enjoy—like having a small "campfire" in the backyard since he could no longer actually go camping (which he loved to do), watching sports together, or looking at old photographs and listening to Papa's stories. We were taking care of the children by letting them take care of us, and in reaching out to comfort them, we were comforted in return. It also gave my husband permission to spend time with each grandchild individually. He told them each something special, and I think they each loved having their private talks and independent memories. This openness and sharing seemed to lessen everyone's discomfort, and the visit turned out to be relaxing and fun—even though we all knew it would be the last one they'd have with Papa.

REX'S STORY

I like taking my five- and seven-year-old boys with me when I visit my ninety-year-old uncle at the nursing home. And, oh my goodness, how my uncle and the other residents light up when those kids come. I always remember being afraid of old people when I was young, but my boys are always eager to go—maybe because my uncle is still pretty sharp, or maybe because we do our best to treat old age as normal. Anyway, the boys love to have jokes or card tricks at the ready, and on our last holiday visit, one of them delighted all of us by asking, "Uncle George, would you like me to teach you how to say 'Happy New Year' in Spanish so you could say it to all your friends here?"

When my fifth-grade daughter's close friend was diagnosed, then hospitalized for leukemia, my daughter was so upset and sad and worried. She wanted to do something special for her friend to cheer her up and to let her know how much all the kids and teachers and parents were missing her and thinking about her. She came up with sending her special messages from everyone who wanted to participate. I helped her make blank notecards out of old greeting cards, and then we cut a piece of colorful fabric to decorate the top, onto which she printed and cut out the words "Hugs in a Jar." Fellow students, school staff, and parents wrote notes, or funny jokes or stories, or found appropriate quotes on the notecards, which my daughter folded and put into the jar to be delivered to her friend at the hospital. Her mother told us how they all loved beginning and ending the day with those "hugs," and I think everyone who took part—especially the children—felt that they were a part of a big circle of love and care.

What other ways can you think of including children in caregiving? Of course, as we've discussed before, each situation is different, as is each caregiver and care receiver. Some children are more mature than others, and some may be too young to participate in a helping activity, so I leave it up to each of you to figure out what activities, if any, seem most appropriate.

The important thing to remember when it comes to fostering compassion and kindness in children is to make sure the messages we give them about values, caring, and kindness are in alignment with our actions. In our interactions with children, we should consistently ask ourselves, "Am I walking the talk?"

Being of Service and Paying It Forward

There's a quotation I've long loved that is usually credited to Shirley Chisholm, an American writer and teacher and the first African

American woman elected to the United States Congress. She said, "Service is the rent we pay for the privilege of living on this earth." Service is also a basic tenet of Twelve Step philosophy:

> By the time we reach Step Twelve, we realize that to maintain our recovery, we can't live in isolation, cut off from the people and things we care about. We have reclaimed our humanity and remembered that to be fully human means to live in community. We have accepted the help that has been given to us, and we have done the hard work of making our recovery program a way of life, one day at a time. We are ready now to give to others what has been given to us.[7]

Some of us might call this "paying it forward," an idea that was popularized in a movie released in 2000 called *Pay It Forward,* in which a young boy urges people to do three good deeds for others when a good deed is done for them. His rationale was that if everyone did this, kindness would spread and the world would become a better place.

Whatever we call the concept, I wholeheartedly believe that compassionate caregiving is a way to be of service, to care for others as we have been (or would like to be) cared for. At its finest, compassionate caregiving is a way to fine-tune our best inner qualities—things like love, patience, tenderness, humor, tolerance, grace, and a capacity for forgiveness—and turn them outward as we do our imperfect best to extend a hand and open our heart to someone in need.

Most of us have children in our lives in some capacity, and I view caring, protecting, and nurturing them a sacred responsibility. When we take time to make time for children, providing them with opportunities and encouragement to practice kindness and caring in their own lives, we expand the whole notion of paying it forward: doing our small but essential part to make our world a more welcoming and loving place for future generations.

. . .

We began this exploration of caregiving by looking within, becoming more self-aware by taking an honest look at which of our caring behaviors might fall on the side of care*taking*, and which were care*giving* behaviors. After reflecting on what messages we've received about caring, we discussed expectations and the importance of healthy balance and boundaries. Then we began to move outward by finding our place in a circle of care and talking about sympathy, empathy, and compassion and how best to compassionately care for ourselves as we take compassionate care of others in a variety of situations, including those times when caregiving "chooses" us. Finally, in this chapter, we complete the caregiving trajectory by focusing on ways we might nurture compassion and kindness in children and how caregiving is a way to pay it forward.

As our journey together comes to its conclusion and your caregiving journeys continue, I want to leave you with a few final reminders:

- We are, all of us, works in progress, united in our imperfection, just trying to do the best job we can. We will have care*taker* days and care*giver* days, but with practice, the scales of care will tilt more toward care*giving* with each experience, so try to have compassion with yourself and patience with the process.

- At those times when you find yourself leaning more toward care*taking*, try doing a random act of kindness. Better yet, try doing an anonymous favor or giving an anonymous gift. It's a great way to get the focus off self and move beyond the need to be needed.

- Try to remain flexible and curious. It is not up to us to fix or save anyone; in fact, sometimes we don't need to say or do anything. We just need to *be* and to listen.

- The more we connect with others, the more caring opportunities we will have, both large and small. Along the way we may encounter some dark days and difficult care receivers.

When that happens, I urge you to get the help and support *you* need in order to maintain healthy balance and boundaries— whether that support is casual or professional. Take heart, take good care, and try to keep a sense of humor. And if anyone tells you "Everything happens for a reason," run away!

- Don't forget about support groups. They can be a rich and wonderful source of *mutual* support. As Martin Luther King Jr. is credited with saying, "We may have all come on different ships, but we're in the same boat now." If no actual support group is available, don't forget about "cyber" friends and online communities. I suggest seeking information and links on the websites of credible organizations that deal with a particular problem, for example, the National Center on Caregiving, Alzheimer's Association, or the National Alliance on Mental Illness. (More sources are listed in the resource section.)

- We aren't alone, so practice asking for help when you need it. And remember about TEAM work—another effective way to move from care*taking* to more balanced care*giving*.

- When you are a primary caregiver, *you* get to choose your support system. When you are necessarily consumed by caregiving responsibilities, try to stay clear of unsupportive people who may unwittingly sabotage your caregiving efforts by trying to control, guilt, shame, or direct you. If you choose, you can reconnect with them when the air clears and the crisis passes.

- Remember to use the tools, techniques, and suggestions in this book. Return to those dog-eared pages and underlined passages whenever the need arises. I also urge you to make copies of the various items in the appendices and keep them handy so you'll have them when you need them.

Always try to remember that you are a caregiver who also deserves to be cared for. Eat healthy, exercise when you can, try your best to minimize stress and maximize rest, and spend time with supportive friends. Laugh and play as often as you are able, and *don't forget to give yourself permission to ask for help.* These things are so important that I have included a Compassionate Caregiver's Contract in appendix G, which I encourage you to copy, fill out, and actually sign. Post it in a place where you'll see it often as a self-care reminder.

I leave you with the words of one of my favorite writers, Anne Lamott:

> Everyone is screwed up, broken, clingy, and scared, even the people who seem to have it more or less together. They are much more like you than you would believe. So try not to compare your insides to their outsides. Also, you can't save, fix, or rescue any of them, or get any of them sober. But radical self-care is quantum, and radiates out into the atmosphere, like a little fresh air. It is a huge gift to the world. When people respond by saying, "Well, isn't she full of herself," smile obliquely, like Mona Lisa, and make both of you a nice cup of tea.[8]

I urge you to take her words to heart. We're all in this together, and it is my sincere hope that you have found the support, guidance, information, and inspiration you need to help you take better care of yourself as you do the honorable work of caring for others.

Epilogue

When I was working on the final chapters of this book, lightning struck three times in my own life. First, I got one of those calls we all dread, the kind that jolts you into immediate caregiver action. This one was from my niece, who called to tell me that her dad—my big brother—had to have a biopsy for a "suspicious spot in his lung." The biopsy confirmed our worst fears: stage III lung cancer, and as I write this he is just beginning a grueling regimen of chemotherapy and radiation.

I do not know what the future holds for my brother, but I am clear, however, about my place in his circle of care. He is blessed to have a wife, six grown children, devoted sons-in-law, and seven grandchildren, so his inner ring is wonderfully full of love and support. While I will, of course, help him in any ways I can, I see my main role as caring for the primary caregivers who occupy the first circle. I am already finding that being so clear about this at the outset helps keep my caretaking tendencies in check.

My next challenge in caring was a little less clear. When Michael, my partner in life and love for over forty-three years, had some heart related health issues that at first looked serious, my caretaking instincts sprang to life as I unsuccessfully fought the urge to control, oversee, and manage his care when he was perfectly capable of managing it himself. Fortunately, I am married to a paragon of patience and understanding who has been with me long enough to know that when I get in my hyper-efficient (also known as controlling!) mode, I am usually acting or reacting out of fear. That's when a Get Out of "Jail" Free card comes in handy, and I played more than one of them during this experience.

I am grateful and relieved to report that all is well, both with his health *and* with our relationship. We worked our way through all the tests, doctors' appointments, and uncertainty together, communicating openly and honestly, using many of the tools I've shared in this book. When we had to rush to the hospital for a CT scan and he didn't want me to call anyone, I worked up the courage to say, "But it's what *I* need; I don't want to wait by myself while you're in there." Michael heard me, and our dear friends immediately came to be with me and to celebrate with both of us when everything came out okay.

The third experience is ongoing as I write this. We learned that a friend whom we hadn't seen for many years died last week. As one person so aptly put it, "He was a good guy who died of a terrible disease." That disease was addiction, and, as is the case with any addiction, the grief it leaves in its wake when it claims a loved one is complex and layered as survivors sift through treasured memories of "when" and mourn what could have been.

Here again, the circle of care concept is working well. Although my husband and I no longer had a close relationship with the person who died, we reached out to help the primary caregivers with whom we do have contact. As a result, we are experiencing a deeper love and connection with them as they, to paraphrase the words of Ernest Hemingway (who sadly wasn't able to benefit from his own wisdom), "grow stronger at the broken places." And that is a good thing. That is the magic that can happen in a compassionate circle of care.

I mention these recent experiences to illustrate how pertinent the things discussed in this book are to real life and how practical the tools can be. While I know that my story is not your story, and that the other stories that caregivers have so generously shared in these pages are unique to them, many of the caregiving issues discussed are common to all of us. I hope you gain some of the same inspiration, comfort, and strength that I have gained from the clear and wise voices in this book. As I said earlier, these are the voices of those who have "been there and done that," so we can trust what they have to say.

Acknowledgments

My heartfelt thanks to all the amazing caregivers who shared their experiences with me, and to those who helped me gather the stories of others. I know how difficult it can be to relive painful events or to talk of them when someone is in the midst of crisis, but those who contributed to this book were so deeply committed to helping others that they did not hesitate. That is the essence of caregiving, and all who read these pages are the beneficiaries of their candor, courage, and wisdom.

Thanks also to Nic and Sue Nicodemus for their contributions and decades of support, and to Lisa Woititz for her cheerful and supportive check-in emails and her spot-on caregiving insights. I also want to acknowledge my many other friends and family members who are always at the ready with a word of encouragement, a listening ear, or an entertaining distraction just when I need it the most.

A special thank-you to the Unity Caregivers, from whom I have gained and learned so much. I love you all and am deeply grateful for your fellowship, your friendship, your profound insights, your raw honesty, your mutual support, the tears, and the humor. It always feels so good to laugh and cry with you! You all helped shape this book.

As always, thanks to Sharon and Rick Slettehaugh who, despite their own caregiving challenges and concerns, took the time to read each and every word I drafted, offering their honest feedback, consistent support, wise counsel, and warm friendship. Oh how I count on those long evenings of conversation and cards!

Ongoing thanks to my longtime writing companion and dear friend, Olivia Gault, whose sharp eye, keen sense of nuance, and immediate grasp of intent have been improving my work for over thirty years. I love our two-person writers' group.

Deep gratitude to Dianna Diers, one of the most perceptive people I know. Just when I needed it the most, she had the uncanny ability to call, saying, "I just wanted to check in to see how you're doing and how I can best support you and your book." Dianna, you've made caregiving an art form—one that you mastered long ago. I thank you for sharing your knowledge of it and your friendship with me.

Sincere thanks to Harriet Barlow, whose friendship I treasure and whose brilliance I so admire. I couldn't ask for a better cheerleader *or* pal. I value your guidance, always appreciate your feedback, and miss our special lunches when you're not here.

A warm thank-you to my sister and close friend, Dianne Smith, one of the bravest and most positive people I know. You've modeled what it means to be a compassionate caregiver in the most difficult of situations. I am so proud of you, and I know that Mom and Dad would be too. Thanks for always being so supportive of me and my writing.

Thanks to my terrific, longtime editor Sid Farrar, whose gentle demeanor, good humor, and friendship make the writing process so painless and enjoyable that I usually don't even mind when he moves up a deadline. Thank you for your confidence and trust, and for helping bring this book to life. Thanks also to production editor April Ebb—the most patient and good-natured "I" dotter and "T" crosser in the business. Your keen eye for detail and exactitude never fails to improve my work.

And my heart overflows with gratitude and love for Michael— my husband, my soul mate, and my constant source of support and inspiration. You make each day brighter and more interesting, each load lighter, each experience richer. And we have so much fun! The world is a better place, and I am a better person, because of you.

Questionnaire for Those Who Give Care

The following questionnaire served as research for this book. I invite you to fill it out as a way to explore or clarify your own caring relationships.

Please key your answers to the number and do not identify anyone by full name.

1. Please respond to any or all of the following statements that describe you when it comes to giving care.

   a. If you are a "caregiver by nature"—someone who has difficulty saying no, or who is often the first to step forward to help someone in need (even when not asked), regardless of your own busy schedule or other commitments—give some examples of times you have "rushed to the rescue."

   b. If you are a "caregiver by choice"—someone who helps friends, family, and/or acquaintances when you are able or when you choose to do so—what are some examples of the types of caregiving activities you engage in? For instance, do you like to make meals, do chores or errands, contribute money, etc., when someone needs help?

   c. If you are (or were) a "caregiver by circumstance"—someone who cares or cared for a loved one because of an accident, illness, surgery, age, addiction, emotional or mental problems, necessity (no one else to help or no money to hire help), etc.—describe the situation and your relationship to the person you care or cared for. Are or were you the primary caregiver? How long have you had (or did you have) this responsibility?

   d. If you are (or were) a caregiver by profession, please describe the nature of your job.

e. Are you a member of a service organization (e.g., school, mutual help group, place of worship, civic organization, etc.) in which you volunteer to help others? Give examples.

2. What are some of the gifts, joys, and/or benefits you have experienced when caring for or helping someone? I invite you to respond with a brief story or example.

3. What are some of the difficulties or challenges you have experienced when caring for or helping someone? Here again, specific examples are great!

4. Has giving care to someone affected or changed your relationship with that person? If so, in what ways?

5. Do you think personal boundaries—the lines and limits that separate *our* views, needs, beliefs, feelings, etc. from someone else's—are important in caring relationships? Why or why not?

6. Have you as a caregiver ever felt you inappropriately crossed a boundary by trying to "fix" a situation or person, trying to take charge when it was not your place to do so, giving more than the situation or person needed or wanted, etc.? Briefly describe such an experience.

7. If caring for a loved one, are you (or were you) able to talk honestly about their goals, needs, desires, abilities, or likely outcome? If not, where would you turn to get the help you need to have such a conversation?

8. Can you give an example of a successful experience in which both caregiver and receiver seemed heard and respected and there was a balance between the help offered and the need for help? What do you think made this relationship work well?

9. Do you often put others' needs before your own? How does this affect your sense of self and role as a caregiver?

10. Have you used alcohol or other drugs to cope with caregiver burnout or stress?

11. Can you tell about a time when you felt overwhelmed with caregiving responsibilities? Did a person or organization help you in some special way?

12. Do you (or did you) have any support systems, beliefs, practices, or special people in your life to help you with the stress and exhaustion that so often accompanies caregiving?

13. What do you do or what do you suggest other caregivers might do when it comes to asking for help or taking care of self?

14. What important lessons have you learned from caregiving?

15. Have your caregiving experiences changed or affected your personal or world view?

Questionnaire for Past or Present Care Receivers

The following questionnaire served as research for this book. I invite you to share it with care recipients or use it as a communication tool when appropriate.

Please key your answers to the number and do not identify anyone by full name.

1. If you are receiving or have received care because of an accident, illness, surgery, other medical condition, age-related difficulties, addiction, emotional or mental problems, death of a loved one, etc.—describe the nature of such care. Feel free to give more than one example of such an instance.

2. Who are (or were) your primary caregiver(s)—e.g., spouse or partner, other family member(s), friend(s), health care professional, volunteers from an organization, etc.

3. How long have you (or did you) require such care?

4. What are some of the gifts, joys, or benefits you experienced when being cared for? I invite you to respond with a brief story or example.

5. What do you feel are the hardest or most frustrating things about asking for or accepting help from others? Here again, specific examples are great!

6. Has being cared for affected your relationship with your primary caregiver(s)? If so, in what ways?

7. What are some of the most helpful things that a caregiver has said or done that made the experience richer or easier?

8. What are some of the most unhelpful things that a caregiver has said or done?

9. Do you think personal boundaries—the lines and limits that separate *our* views, needs, beliefs, feelings, etc. from someone else's—are important in caring relationships? Why or why not?

10. Have you ever felt your caregiver(s) inappropriately or inadvertently crossed a boundary by trying to "fix" you or a situation, trying to take charge when it was not their place to do so, or giving more than you needed or wanted, etc.? If so, briefly describe such an experience.

11. Are you or were you able to be open and honest with your caregivers? If not, why not?

12. Are you or were you able to talk honestly with your spouse, partner, close friend, relative, or companion about your feelings, goals, hopes, fears, frustrations, needs, or desires? If not, where do you think you could turn to get the help you need to have such a conversation?

13. Do you or did you feel listened to and really heard when you try or tried to express your feelings while receiving care?

14. Can you give an example of a successful experience in which both you and a caregiver seemed heard and respected and there was a balance between the help offered and the need for help? What do you think made this relationship work well?

15. Do you (or did you) have any support systems, beliefs, practices, or special people in your life that help or helped you as a care receiver?

16. What would you like or have liked your caregiver(s) to know or understand about caring for you or someone else?

17. What important lessons have you learned from the experience of receiving care?

18. Has the experience of needing and accepting care from others affected or changed your self-image or the way you view others?

Some Common Characteristics of Caretakers and Caregivers

Caretakers	Caregivers
Often need to be needed	Want to be of help
Have a need or desire to fix	Support others in problem solving
Like to be the "special one"	Are usually good team players
Often try to control a person or situation	Are content to be helpers
Often try to manipulate	Try to cooperate
Often struggle with low self-esteem	Usually have a healthy sense of self
Often overstep or disregard boundaries	Respect boundaries (their own and others')
Have difficulty saying no	Can gracefully decline an invitation or request when it is necessary to do so
Tend to put others' needs above their own	Practice good self-care
Are often judgmental and critical	Are usually accepting and nonjudgmental
Often feel responsible for others' needs and feelings	Understand that they are only responsible for their *own* actions and feelings
Often "give to get"—i.e., help others out of a need to be thanked, liked, accepted, etc.	Act out of compassion and concern for others with no "strings attached"
Often have difficulty making decisions	Are not usually second-guessers

Caretakers	Caregivers
Frequently have lives out of balance	Try to live a balanced life
Are often "people pleasers"	Have a healthy respect for self *and* others
Are often poor listeners	Are usually attentive and "active" listeners
Have trouble setting and honoring priorities	Try to set and maintain priorities
Are often resentful	Are usually grateful
Often adopt an attitude of self-sacrifice	Try to maintain a spirit of generosity
Frequently lavish praise on others	Are genuine in their admiration and praise
Have a tendency to get overly involved in another person's life or problems	Maintain appropriate boundaries
Often offer advice or help without being asked	Maintain appropriate boundaries
Often have "uneven," one-up/ one-down relationships	Thrive on healthy relationships that have a good balance of "give and take"
Often assume they know what's best; are invested in being right regarding someone's care choices and may argue their point of view (even when they weren't asked for their opinion)	Respect another's opinions and choices and accept that person's decisions about their own care (even though they may disagree with them)

Circle of Care

Here is a template for creating your own circle of care. (See the instructions on page 85.)

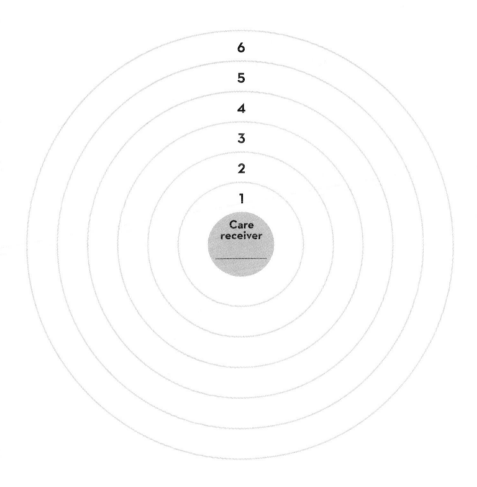

Obstacles to Self-Care: A Brief Review

Many of the care*taker* characteristics discussed in this book can also be seen as behaviors that can interfere with caring for ourselves while we're caring for others. The following chart lists some of these characteristics seen through the lens of self-care, together with a suggested remedy that might open the door to better self-care:

Possible obstacle to self-care	Suggested remedy
Needing to be the "special one" (defining our worth by how we think others need us) leaves little time for reflection and self-care.	Finding our appropriate place in a circle of care helps us share care responsibilities with someone else in our "ring," which gives us more time for self-care.
Wanting to be the perfect caregiver can lead to doing too much "other care" and not enough self-care.	Embracing our imperfection leaves room for self-care and helps prevent a "one-up/one-down" relationship.
Having unreal or unmet expectations can lead to disappointment, depression, and poor self-care.	Accepting what we cannot change and watching out for the "if only," "should," or "always/never" messages we send ourselves can reduce stress and resentment, increasing our ability to care for others as we care for ourselves.
Believing messages about the "duty" of caregiving and the importance of others can discourage us from caring for ourselves because we were taught it is selfish to tend to our own needs before we help others.	Sifting through *both* positive and negative caregiving messages for those who serve us well can lead to more compassionate caregiving and a healthier approach to self-care.
Having inappropriate boundaries can turn a casual offer of help into an all-consuming care situation, leaving little time for self-care.	Setting and maintaining healthy boundaries helps us better assess a caregiving commitment to see what areas of *our* lives could be adversely affected.

Possible obstacle to self-care	Suggested remedy
Having "unboundaried" empathy can cause us to get so consumed and tangled up with someone's problems and feelings that *we* get adversely affected (e.g., stressed or depressed), which can put our well-being and self-care at risk.	"Emptying our own cup" beforehand helps us establish appropriate boundaries so we can be fully present and more aware of a traumatized person's emotions versus our reactions to *their* story, which helps us take better care of ourselves in emotionally challenging caregiving situations.

When you read through self-care obstacles and remedies listed in this chart, you'll notice how they ultimately direct us to the importance of self-care in caregiving. If, when reading through the list, you have that "Ouch; this still strikes a chord" reaction to one of the obstacles or suggested remedies, I encourage you to revisit the relevant sections in the book for more detailed discussion of that issue or issues.

Get Out of "Jail" Free Cards

Compassionate Caregiving

GET OUT OF "JAIL" FREE

Use this card when needed.

Compassionate Caregiving

GET OUT OF "JAIL" FREE

Use this card when needed.

Compassionate Caregiving

GET OUT OF "JAIL" FREE

Use this card when needed.

Compassionate Caregiver's Contract

This is intended as a contract for you to print, fill out, and post somewhere to remind yourself that you need to take compassionate care of yourself as you care for others.

I, _____

recognize that I am a caregiver who also deserves to be cared for and nurtured to promote my overall mental health and physical well-being. I promise to do my best to do the following things to care for myself so that I can continue to care for others* (add to this list as needed):

1. _____

2. _____

3. _____

4. _____

5. _____

6. _____

7. _____

Signed _____

Date _____ / _____ / _____

* Your list could include things like eating healthy foods regularly, trying not to stress out about little things, enjoying time for yourself, sleeping more, exercising, spending time with friends, or giving yourself permission to ask for help.

In Case of Emergency (ICE) Card

In Case of Emergency

Medical emergency information for:

Name: _____

Address: _____

Phone: _____

Emergency contacts

❶ Name: _____ ↓fold here

    Relationship: _____

    Phone: _____

❷ Name: _____

    Relationship: _____

    Phone: _____

Insurance company: _____

Phone: _____

☐ Insurance cards in wallet.

Primary physician: _____ ↓fold here

Phone: _____

Medical conditions: _____

_____

Blood type: _____

Allergies: _____

Medications: _____

_____

Resources

Websites for Caregiving Information, Support, and Resources

Family Caregiver Alliance (FCA)/National Center on Caregiving

www.caregiver.org; 1-800-445-8106

In addition to an extensive library of fact sheets, articles, checklists, webinars, and videos on caregiving issues, FCA offers a state-by-state Family Care Navigator at its website to help family caregivers locate public, nonprofit, and private programs and services nearest their loved one—living at home or in a residential facility. Resources include government health and disability programs, legal resources, disease-specific organizations, and more (www.caregiver .org/family-care-navigator).

Caregiver Action Network

www.caregiveraction.org

Caregiver Action Network provides education, peer support, accessible tools, and resources to assist caregivers in managing the care of their loved ones.

National Alliance for Caregiving (NAC)

www.caregiving.org

NAC is a nonprofit coalition of national organizations that focus on advancing family caregiving through research, innovation, and advocacy. It develops national best-practice programs and works to increase public awareness of family caregiving issues.

Rosalynn Carter Institute for Caregiving

www.rosalynncarter.org

The overall goal of the Rosalynn Carter Institute for Caregiving is to support caregivers—both family and professional—through efforts of advocacy, education, research, and service.

AARP

www.aarp.org

AARP is a nonprofit, nonpartisan organization with a membership of nearly 38 million that deals with issues that matter most to families—such as health care, employment and income security, and protection from financial abuse. AARP's Caregiving Resource Center offers up-to-date, expert advice and resources on caregiving issues and concerns (www.aarp.org/home-family/caregiving).

U.S. Administration on Aging Eldercare Locator

www.eldercare.gov/Eldercare.NET/Public/Index.aspx

This is an easy-to-use, free public service that can connect caregivers to services for older adults and their families in their area. Caregivers simply put in their zip code and select the kind of services they are looking for on the drop-down menu. You can also call 1-800-677-1116.

Medicare Caregiver Resource Kit

www.medicare.gov/campaigns/caregiver/caregiver-resource-kit.html

This section of the "Ask Medicare" tool kit offers informational resources that can be printed directly from the website and provided to caregivers. The resources are designed to help caregivers address challenging issues and work effectively with Medicare to ensure their family members and friends receive the best possible care.

Alzheimer's Association

www.alz.org

Formed in 1980, the Alzheimer's Association is the world's leading voluntary health organization in Alzheimer's care, support, and research. It provides an easy-to-use interactive map to help

caregivers find support and services in their area (www.alz.org/apps
/findus.asp). It also provides a 24/7 help line phone number at
1-800-272-3900.

U.S. Department of Health and Human Services Caregiver Resources

www.hhs.gov/aging/long-term-care/index.html
Caregivers can find links to a vast amount of information regarding caregiver resources and information on long-term care at this website.

National Alliance on Mental Illness (NAMI)

www.nami.org
In addition to a wealth of information about various mental illnesses, NAMI has a separate section for family members and those who care for someone with a mental illness (www.nami.org/Find-Support /Family-Members-and-Caregivers).

Substance Abuse and Mental Health Services Administration (SAMHSA)

www.samhsa.gov
This government agency provides good information and links on mental health and substance abuse.

Alcohol, Drug, and Codependency Websites for Information and Support

Al-Anon

www.al-anon.alateen.org; 1-888-4AL-ANON
A Twelve Step organization for loved ones of chemically dependent people.

Alcoholics Anonymous

www.aa.org

A Twelve Step organization for substance abusers.

Nar-Anon

www.nar-anon.org

A Twelve Step organization for loved ones of addicts.

SAMHSA Substance Abuse Treatment Facility Locator

www.findtreatment.samhsa.gov

Connects individuals to treatment facilities in their area.

Books You Might Find Helpful, Enjoyable, or Inspirational

Self-Care, Caregiving, and Inspiration

No Saints around Here: A Caregiver's Days by Susan Allen Toth (Minneapolis: University of Minnesota Press, 2014). A poignant, often funny, and always honest book written by a caregiver about the joys and difficulties of caring for a loved one with a serious illness.

Being Mortal: Medicine and What Matters in the End by Atul Gawande (New York: Metropolitan Books / Henry Holt, 2014). A helpful, informative, and honest look at end-of-life care and challenges in this country by a surgeon who distinguishes between a good *life* and a good *death*.

Stitches: A Handbook on Meaning, Hope and Repair by Anne Lamott (New York: Riverhead Books / Penguin Group, 2013). A wise, funny, and inspirational book for when our lives get out of balance.

Help, Thanks, Wow: The Three Essential Prayers by Anne Lamott (New York: Riverhead Books / Penguin Group, 2013). Three meditations on asking for help, appreciating the good we witness, and feeling awe in the world, written in Lamott's usual profound and funny style.

Shock Waves: A Practical Guide to Living with a Loved One's PTSD by Cynthia Orange (Center City, MN: Hazelden Publishing, 2010). A book that shows what PTSD looks like in real life and how important it is for families to take care of themselves as they care for their loved one with PTSD.

Gratitude by Oliver Sacks (New York: Alfred A. Knopf, 2015). A beautiful little book written about illness and death by a man in the last months of his life.

Addiction and Codependency

Codependent No More: How to Stop Controlling Others and Start Caring for Yourself by Melody Beattie (Center City, MN: Hazelden Publishing, 1987, 1992). The "bible" of codependency by the author who coined the term.

Playing It by Heart: Taking Care of Yourself No Matter What by Melody Beattie (Center City, MN: Hazelden Publishing, 1999). Personal essays and guidance about codependency.

If You Leave Me, Can I Come with You? by Misti B. (Center City, MN: Hazelden Publishing, 2015). A humorous yet honest daily meditation book for codependents.

Unwelcome Inheritance: Break Your Family's Cycle of Addictive Behaviors by Lisa Sue Woititz and Dr. Janet G. Woititz (Center City, MN: Hazelden Publishing, 2015). Shows how addictions can be passed from one generation to the next. Good information on codependency.

Recovery Now: A Basic Text for Today by Anonymous (Center City, MN: Hazelden Publishing, 2013). An accessible basic text written in today's language for anyone guided by the Twelve Steps in recovering from addiction to alcohol or other drugs.

Notes

Introduction

1. Peggi Speers and Tia Walker, *The Inspired Caregiver: Finding Joy While Caring for Those You Love* (North Charleston, SC: CreateSpace Independent Publishing Platform, 2013).
2. *Caregiving in the U.S. 2015* (National Alliance for Caregiving and the AARP Public Policy Institute, June 2015), www.aarp.org/content/dam/aarp/ppi/2015/caregiving-in-the-united-states-2015-report-revised.pdf.
3. Pat Donovan, "Study Finds It Actually Is Better (and Healthier) to Give Than to Receive," University at Buffalo, news release, February 4, 2013, www.buffalo.edu/news/releases/2013/02/003.html.

Chapter 1

1. Anne Wilson Schaef, meditation for January 31 in *Meditations for Women Who Do Too Much* (San Francisco: Harper and Row, 1990).
2. David D. Burns, *Feeling Good: The New Mood Therapy*, revised and updated ed. (New York: Avon Books, 1999).
3. Melody Beattie, *Codependent No More: How to Stop Controlling Others and Start Caring for Yourself* (Center City, MN: Hazelden Publishing, 1987, 1992).
4. Ibid., 84–85.
5. Ibid., 85.
6. Ibid., 90.

Chapter 2

1. Anne Lamott, *Stitches: A Handbook on Meaning, Hope and Repair* (New York: Riverhead Books / Penguin Group, 2013).
2. Lynn Friss Feinberg and Carol Levine, "Family Caregiving: Looking to the Future," American Society on Aging (blog), January 1, 2016, www.asaging.org/blog/family-caregiving

-looking-future. Originally published in the Winter 2015/2016 issue of the American Society on Aging's journal *Generations*.

3. Ibid.

4. Lori L. Jervis, Mathew E. Boland, and Alexandra Fickenscher, "American Indian Family Caregivers' Experiences with Helping Elders," *Journal of Cross-Cultural Gerontology* 25, no. 4 (2010): 355–369, doi: 10.1007/s10823-010-9131-9.

5. Ibid.

6. American Psychological Association, "Cultural Diversity and Caregiving," January 2011, www.apa.org/pi/about/publications /caregivers/faq/cultural-diversity.aspx.

7. Phillip Moffitt, "The Tyranny of Expectations," http:// dharmawisdom.org/teachings/articles/tyranny-expectations.

8. *Recovery Now: A Basic Text for Today* (Center City, MN: Hazelden Publishing, 2013), 68.

Chapter 3

1. Misti B., *If You Leave Me, Can I Come with You?* (Center City, MN: Hazelden Publishing, 2015), 12.

2. Salvador Minuchin, *Families & Family Therapy* (Cambridge, MA: Harvard University Press, 1974), 54.

3. Viktor E. Frankl, *Man's Search for Meaning* (Boston: Beacon Press, 1959).

Chapter 4

1. Jeffrey Goldberg, "Jonathan Safran Foer on the Morality of Vegetarianism," *The Atlantic*, December 11, 2009, www .theatlantic.com/international/archive/2009/12/jonathan -safran-foer-on-the-morality-of-vegetarianism/31686.

2. Susan Allen Toth, *No Saints around Here: A Caregiver's Days* (Minneapolis: University of Minnesota Press, 2014), 159–160.

3. Susan Silk and Barry Goldman, "How Not to Say the Wrong Thing," *Los Angeles Times*, April 7, 2013, http://articles.latimes .com/2013/apr/07/opinion/la-oe-0407-silk-ring-theory -20130407.

4. Ibid.

5. Ibid.

6. Christina Baldwin, *Storycatcher: Making Sense of Our Lives through the Power and Practice of Story* (Novato, CA: New World Library, 2005).

7. Adapted from Cynthia Orange, *Shock Waves: A Practical Guide to Living with a Loved One's PTSD* (Center City, MN: Hazelden Publishing, 2010), 93–95.

8. Found at the Fred Rogers Company website, www.fredrogers .org/parents/special-challenges/tragic-events.php.

Chapter 5

1. From "The Nature of Healing with Stephen Levine," an interview by Jeffrey Mishlove with Stephen Levine on the *Thinking Allowed, Conversations on the Leading Edge of Knowledge and Discovery* television series on the Intuition Network. Transcript of the program found at www.intuition.org/txt/levine.htm.

2. Brené Brown, interview by Travis Reed, *Independence vs. Need,* film, www.theworkofthepeople.com/independence-vs-need

3. Cynthia Orange, *Shock Waves: A Practical Guide to Living with a Loved One's PTSD* (Center City, MN: Hazelden Publishing, 2010), 45.

4. "What Is Empathy?" University of California, Berkeley Greater Good Science Center newsletter (undated), http://greatergood .berkeley.edu/topic/empathy/definition.

5. "How Well Do You Read Other People?" Body Language Quiz: Test Your Emotional Intelligence, developed by University of California, Berkeley Greater Good Science Center, http:// greatergood.berkeley.edu/ei_quiz.

6. Charles Siebert, "What Does a Parrot Know about PTSD?" *New York Times Magazine,* January 28, 2016, www.nytimes .com/2016/01/31/magazine/what-does-a-parrot-know-about -ptsd.html?_r=0.

7. "What Is Empathy?" University of California, Berkeley Greater
   Good Science Center newsletter (undated), http://greatergood
   .berkeley.edu/topic/empathy/definition.

8. Brené Brown, interview by Travis Reed, *Independence vs. Need*,
   film, www.theworkofthepeople.com/independence-vs-need.

9. Keely Chace, "What to Write in a Sympathy Card: Sympathy
   Card Message Ideas from Hallmark writers," Hallmark website,
   http://ideas.hallmark.com/sympathy-ideas/what-to-write-in-a
   -sympathy-card.

Chapter 6

1. Julie Beck, "The Internet Wants to Help You Take Care of
   Yourself," *The Atlantic*, October 15, 2015, www.theatlantic.com
   /health/archive/2015/10/internet-self-care/408580/.

2. Pat Donovan, "Study Finds It Actually Is Better (and Healthier)
   to Give Than to Receive," University at Buffalo, news release,
   February 4, 2013, www.buffalo.edu/news/releases/2013/02
   /003.html.

3. Corporation for National and Community Service, Office of
   Research and Policy Development, *The Health Benefits of Volunteering: A Review of Recent Research* (Washington, DC: Corporation for National and Community Service, Office of Research
   and Policy Development, 2007), www.nationalservice.gov/pdf
   /07_0506_hbr.pdf.

4. Ibid., 13.

5. Ibid., 8.

6. Ibid., 5.

7. Susan Allen Toth, *No Saints around Here: A Caregiver's Days*
   (Minneapolis: University of Minnesota Press, 2014), 47.

8. Ibid., 48.

9. Found at Kristin Neff's website, www.self-compassion.org.

10. Kristin Neff, "Definition of Self-Compassion," www.self
    -compassion.org.

11. Kristin Neff, "Self-Compassion Is Not Self-Esteem," www.self
    -compassion.org.

12. Julie Beck, "The Internet Wants to Help You Take Care of Yourself," *The Atlantic,* October 15, 2015, www.theatlantic.com /health/archive/2015/10/internet-self-care/408580/.

Chapter 7

1. Mark Nepo, *The Book of Awakenings,* gift ed. (San Francisco: Conari Press, 2011), 364.
2. Excerpted from Tom Peek, "What I Learned from the Dayton's Bombing," TwinCities.com—*Pioneer Press,* updated September 16, 2010, http://tompeek.net/docs/dayton.htm.
3. Family Caregiver Alliance, "Taking Care of YOU: Self-Care for Family Caregivers," revised 2012, www.caregiver.org/taking -care-you-self-care-family-caregivers.

Chapter 8

1. "A Conversation with George Hodgman," http://georgehodgman .com/a-conversation-with-george-hodgman.
2. National Institute on Aging, "About Alzheimer's Disease: Alzheimer's Basics," www.nia.nih.gov/alzheimers/topics /alzheimers-basics.
3. Mayo Clinic staff, "Dementia," www.mayoclinic.org/diseases -conditions/dementia/symptoms-causes/dxc-20198504.
4. Ibid.
5. National Institute on Aging, "About Alzheimer's Disease: Alzheimer's Basics," www.nia.nih.gov/alzheimers/topics /alzheimers-basics.
6. National Alliance on Mental Illness, "Mental Health Conditions," www.nami.org/Learn-More/Mental-Health-Conditions.
7. National Alliance on Mental Illness, "Family Members and Caregivers," www.nami.org/Find-Support/Family-Members -and-Caregivers.
8. *Recovery Now: A Basic Text for Today* (Center City, MN: Hazelden Publishing, 2013).
9. Ibid., 147–148.

10. The Conversation Project, www.theconversationproject.org.
11. Family Caregiver Alliance, "Caregiving and Sibling Relationships: Challenges and Opportunities," www.caregiver.org /print/235.
12. Ibid.

Chapter 9
1. L. R. Knost, *Two Thousand Kisses a Day: Gentle Parenting Through the Ages and Stages* (Little Heart Books, 2013).
2. The President and Fellows of Harvard College, "The Children We Mean to Raise: The Real Messages Adults Are Sending about Values," Making Caring Common Project, Harvard Graduate School of Education, 2014, http://mcc.gse.harvard.edu /the-children-we-mean-to-raise.
3. Ibid.
4. Ibid.
5. Ibid.
6. Nancy Shute, "Random Acts of Kindness Can Make Kids More Popular," National Public Radio, December 27, 2012, www.npr .org/sections/health-shots/2012/12/27/168128084/random -acts-of-kindness-can-make-kids-more-popular.
7. *Recovery Now: A Basic Text for Today* (Center City, MN: Hazelden Publishing, 2013), 107–108.
8. Anne Lamott's Facebook page, April 8, 2015, www.facebook .com/AnneLamott/posts/662177577245222.

About the Author

Cynthia Orange is a writer, editor, and writing consultant. Her books include *Shock Waves: A Practical Guide to Living with a Loved One's PTSD* (Hazelden Publishing, 2010) and *Sing Your Own Song* (Hazelden Publishing, 2001), and she is the coauthor of *New Life, New Friends* (Bantam, 1993) and a contributor to *Today's Gift* (Hazelden Publishing, 1985). She has received awards for creative nonfiction, poetry, essays, and newspaper articles.

Orange co-facilitates a group for caregivers of a variety of ages and circumstances that was founded in 2010. She has written extensively about caregiving and post-traumatic stress disorder, and she and her husband, Michael, a Vietnam combat veteran, often speak to audiences about the effects of trauma and war in their continuing involvement with veterans and veterans' issues.

About Hazelden Publishing

As part of the Hazelden Betty Ford Foundation, Hazelden Publishing offers both cutting-edge educational resources and inspirational books. Our print and digital works help guide individuals in treatment and recovery, and their loved ones. Professionals who work to prevent and treat addiction also turn to Hazelden Publishing for evidence-based curricula, digital content solutions, and videos for use in schools, treatment programs, correctional programs, and electronic health records systems. We also offer training for implementation of our curricula.

Through published and digital works, Hazelden Publishing extends the reach of healing and hope to individuals, families, and communities affected by addiction and related issues.

For more information about Hazelden publications,
please call **800-328-9000**
or visit us online at **hazelden.org/bookstore**.

Other titles that may interest you:

Shock Waves
A Practical Guide to Living with a Loved One's PTSD
Cynthia Orange

Shock Waves is a user-friendly guide for those who love someone suffering from PTSD. Readers find practical insights on how to respond to substance abuse and other co-occurring disorders, manage their reactions to a loved one's rage, find effective professional help, and prevent their children from experiencing secondary trauma.

Order No. 2602; e-book EB2602

If You Leave Me, Can I Come with You?
Daily Meditations for Codependents and Al-Anons . . .
with a Sense of Humor
Misti B.

If You Leave Me, Can I Come with You? is full of refreshingly original meditations for each day of the year. Infusing her wisdom with self-revealing honesty and humor, Misti B. provides healing insight with a lighthearted touch into the common struggles that codependents and those in Al-Anon frequently face.

Order No. 4828; e-book EB4828

Codependent No More
How to Stop Controlling Others and Start Caring for Yourself
Melody Beattie

With instructive life stories, personal reflections, exercises, and self-tests, *Codependent No More* is a simple, straightforward, readable map of the perplexing world of codependency.

Order No. 5014; e-book EB5014

For more information about Hazelden Publishing publications,
please call **800-328-9000**
or visit us online at **hazelden.org/bookstore**.